Journey with the Holy Spirit

Experience great joys moving in Christ Jesus

ANGELA SCOTT SIMPSON

LAURUS BOOKS

Scripture taken from (ONM) The One New Man Bible, copyright © 2011 William J. Morford. Used by permission of True Potential Publishing, Inc.

Scripture quotations marked (NLT) are taken from the Holy Bible, New Living Translation, copyright © 1996, 2004, 2007, 2013, 2015 by Tyndale House Foundation. Used by permission of Tyndale House Publishers, Inc., Carol Stream, Illinois 60188. All rights reserved.

Scripture quotations are from the ESV® Bible (The Holy Bible, English Standard Version®), copyright © 2001 by Crossway, a publishing ministry of Good News Publishers. Used by permission. All rights reserved.

Scripture is taken from GOD'S WORD®, © 1995 God's Word to the Nations. Used by permission of Baker Publishing Group.

THE HOLY BIBLE, NEW INTERNATIONAL VERSION®, NIV® Copyright © 1973, 1978, 1984, 2011 by Biblica, Inc.® Used by permission. All rights reserved worldwide.

Scripture taken from the NEW AMERICAN STANDARD BIBLE®, Copyright © 1960,1962,1963,1968, 1971, 1972,1973,1975,1977,1995 by The Lockman Foundation. Used by permission.

Quotes from the Complete Jewish Bible by David H. Stern. Copyright © 1998. All rights reserved. Used by permission of Messianic Jewish Publishers, 6120 Day Long Lane, Clarksville, MD 21029. www.messianicjewish.net.

Scripture quotations marked HCSB are taken from the Holman Christian Standard Bible®, Copyright © 1999, 2000, 2002, 2003, 2009 by Holman Bible Publishers. Used by permission. Holman Christian Standard Bible®, Holman CSB®, and HCSB® are federally registered trademarks of Holman Bible Publishers.

The Authorized (King James) Version of the Bible ('the KJV'), the rights in which are vested in the Crown in the United Kingdom, is reproduced here by permission of the Crown's patentee, Cambridge University Press. The King James Version of the Bible (KJV) is public domain in the United States.

Journey With The Holy Spirit
By Angela Scott Simpson

Copyright © 2018 Angela Scott Simpson

No part of this book may be reproduced in any form or by any means, electronic or mechanical, including photocopying, recording, or by storage and retrieval system, without written permission from The Laurus Company, Inc. and the author.

ISBN 978-1-943523-39-9 Paperback Book
ISBN 978-1-943523-40-5 Kindle
ISBN 978-1-943523-41-2 ePub (iBooks, Nook)

Published by LAURUS BOOKS

LAURUS BOOKS
www.TheLaurusCompany.com

Laurus Books is an imprint of The Laurus Company, Inc. This book may be ordered in paperback from TheLaurusCompany.com, Amazon.com, Barnes and Noble, Spring Arbor, and other retailers around the world. Also available in formats for electronic readers from their respective stores.

JOURNEY WITH THE HOLY SPIRIT

Table of Contents

	Introduction: Why I wrote this book	9
1	Astonishing Savior Who changed our living situation	11
2	Excruciating pain caused Pearl to call on Jesus	14
3	Assured seven-year-old orator	16
4	Start, then God will help you with the rest	18
5	Grace and mercy told her what we needed	20
6	Salvation rescued a friend	22
7	Jesus gave me breath to praise Him	26
8	A divine secret message from the Holy Spirit	28
9	You told her about "Me"	31
10	Thank God, I forgave the handyman	34
11	Jesus excellently sustains	37
12	I saw God in Utah	40
13	Gladly obeyed Holy Spirit in Arkansas	43
14	Jesus keeps an eye on His sheep	46
15	A sword raised for surgery	48
16	A love letter to Great-Grandmother	50
17	Increased worship to receive manifested plans	52
18	I found a loving dad in a father-in-law	54
19	Stand at attention! Bold message showed me who I am	58
20	The beginning of creation brought worship and true love	61
21	God gave me great news for my future	63
22	A Christmas blessing from our grandbaby, Elizabeth	65
23	Mercy protected us	67
24	Jesus' peace saved the day	70
25	Salvation at Sunset River Hotel	73
26	Bought laptop case, then received laptop by faith	76
27	A memorable character of Jesus revealed through a smile	78
28	Jesus' love expressed in local store	80

Table of Contents

29	Forever grateful for Jesus' protection	83
30	Never assume they won't be ready to share Christ	85
31	Thankfulness got Jesus' attention	87
32	Listen, the Holy Spirit is talking	89
33	No strangers in the body of Christ	91
34	Love won, rebellion lost	93
35	A thankful heart transformed their heart	96
36	Each one reach one	99
37	Jesus did not blame my shame	101
38	Holy Spirit revealed plans	103
39	Taste a little salt	106
40	Favorable revelation illuminated my spirit	108
41	Reminder of love in sadness	110
42	Do as I do	112
43	Discovered family	113
44	Grandmother gave glory to Jesus	116
45	Marsha's unstoppable faith	117
46	Offense, I send you away	120
47	Jesus, a successful Author	122
48	Early morning truth responded	123
49	Perfect way for our husbands	125
50	First Class information	127
51	God's directions are well lit	128
52	Choose a word, make it good	130
53	My name carried my purpose	131
54	Know who I AM, and know who I am not	133
55	Follow fruitfulness, leave artificial food behind	134
56	Let me put on the Holy Spirit Son glasses	135
57	Memory Lane not worth remembering	139
58	Love keeps us waiting for His coming	141

Table of Contents

59	Come, get on the fantastic voyage	142
60	A free ride settled by Jesus	143
61	Stop your plans. Ask for Mine.	146
62	Never bow. Stand.	147
63	Morning word makes our days brighter	149
64	Speak good fruit	151
65	Trust God searching for unfamiliar work	153
66	Testimonies bring our listeners to the feet of Jesus	155
67	NOW GO, Angela. I AM is with your mouth!	157
68	A wink brought laughter	160
69	Move and finish	162
70	Your heart from God's point of view	164
71	Downloading the Word of God	166
72	Be ready for your Bridegroom	168
73	Pleasing Jesus has become my affection	170
74	A monumental word	171
75	Rain held for my safety	174
76	Lovingly obliged word	175
77	Wowed by His thoughtfulness	176
78	God rewards private work	177
79	Journeyed reflection	178
80	God's Word has your best interest	181
81	Magnificence revealed from God's spoken word	183
82	Healing was done for me, too	185
83	I clearly see His sent Word	187
84	The Spirit of Truth gives what I need to move forward	189
85	Jesus' will is above distractions	190
86	A hardened heart does not stop God's purpose	192
87	Living in Jesus' perfect truth	195
88	Hallelujah time in the parking lot	197

Table of Contents

89	Truth drove anxiousness out	199
90	A prayer blessed someone in the breakroom	201
91	Trials build godly character	203
92	Patience opens doors	204
93	Stop at the counsel of God	206
94	Jesus' presence dispatches His plans	208
95	Heart changed through a lost	209
96	Reminds me that He abides	211
97	Boldness is me	213
98	Living through Christ's mindset	214
99	You are waiting on me and no one else	216
100	Personal prescription given by the Holy Spirit	217
101	Healing during closing hours	219
102	Cancer has no residence in the Kingdom	221
103	Aroma of love to the unkind	223
104	In Him is treasure	225
105	Your insecurities have no power	226
106	Stolen tag brought forgiveness	228
107	Guilt blinded, love made me see	230
108	Everlasting is peace	232
109	Promotion in a fiery furnace	234
110	Loving from a renewed heart	236
111	Christ Jesus, our high position	237
112	Opportunities begin with repentance	238
113	Jesus is exceedingly more	239
Epilogue		242
About the Author		243

Introduction
Why I wrote this book

I wrote this book because I wanted God's chosen ones to know that He is always with them. The Holy Spirit is always there to speak to you. He is there to guide you in every area of your life without question. How sweet it is to hear the voice of the Holy Spirit directing you.

To journey with the Holy Spirit gives you confidence and comforts you along the way. When I spend time listening to the Holy Spirit, it is as if I am sitting right in front of Him with focused attention and open ears, not wanting to miss anything that is being revealed to me.

Before retiring for bed, I always feel an urgency to meet with the Holy Spirit for a private conference with just Him and me discussing all necessary things I need to know that are pleasing to Him. When the Holy Spirit and I meet privately, it is sometimes hard to contain my quietness because of the wisdom and love He shares with me. Even when it is a conviction of love, I know it is for my good, since He knows my purpose for this life here on earth.

The Holy Spirit is my guiding light, and knowing He is there assures my steps when I obey His instructions. Knowing I can trust the Holy Spirit in my stormy experiences turns those experiences into peace that definitely surpasses my understanding. So enjoy the presence of the Holy Spirit. He is our Teacher and makes His time available for us to hear His illuminated Word.

---

1 John 2:26-27 (ONM): I wrote these things to you about those who deceive you. And about the anointing of the Holy Spirit, which you took from Him, which remains in you, and you do not need someone to teach you, but as this anointing for the gifts of the Spirit teaches you about all things and is true and is not a lie, so just as He taught you, remain in Him.

1

Astonishing Savior
Who changed our living situation

The way our Savior, Jesus Christ, provided for us in November 2011 was absolutely astonishing. We had to vacate our home after eight years of living there. Our businesses were not bringing in enough money, and jobs were scarce because of the city where we lived. We did not have enough income to maintain residence in the home, and it became evident that our circumstances would not allow us to keep it. What was alarming about our situation was that we did not have enough money to move to another place. We seemed to be up against an immovable wall.

We knew we had to be proactive to be able to gather enough money to move into another place. Then something remarkable and unprecedented happened that only our Heavenly Father could have planned in this seemingly impossible situation.

My husband Elliott and I met a gentleman at an actor's gathering. My husband is an aspiring actor who has appeared in several movies. We decided to go to an actor's meeting because my husband said maybe he could reach out to people and ask them if they knew anyone who was hiring. Arriving at the actor's meeting, we stood around meeting people. My husband and I split up for a while to meet other aspiring actors and actresses. A couple of hours passed when suddenly my husband hurried toward me with a gentleman who said he might be able to help us. He told us about an opening at a condo complex where we could live for free and manage the upkeep of the buildings. My husband and I thought about it and decided to look into it. We set up an interview with one of the owners. Knowing our living and foreclosure situation, he asked us during the interview if we knew about the cash for keys program. We said no, so the owner proceeded to explain the steps of how to get the cash for keys. Elliott and I went for it. We called the broker who was handling everything concerning our home. The broker set up a time he wanted us to vacate the premises. The house had to be immaculately clean when we turned in the keys in order to get the cash. It took a lot of work, but it was worth it.

We decided not to take the job we had interviewed for because of personal reasons, but look how Jesus opened the door for us. Jesus made provisions for us to move when we had hardly nothing. Jesus went ahead of us as He did with Jehoshaphat who found the armies dead upon arriving at the battleground.

---

2 Chronicles 20:9 (NLT): "They said, 'Whenever we are faced with any calamity such as war, plague, or famine, we can come to stand in your presence before this Temple where your name is honored. We can cry out to you to save us, and you will hear us and rescue us.' "

2 Chronicles 20:21-26 (NLT):
21: After consulting the people, the king appointed singers to walk ahead of the army, singing to the Lord and praising him for his holy splendor. This is what they sang: "Give thanks to the Lord; his faithful love endures forever!"
22: At the very moment they began to sing and give praise, the Lord caused the armies of Ammon, Moab, and Mount Seir to start fighting among themselves.
23: The armies of Moab and Ammon turned against their allies from Mount Seir and killed every one of them. After they had destroyed the army of Seir, they began attacking each other.
24: So when the army of Judah arrived at the lookout point in the wilderness, all they saw were dead bodies lying on the ground as far as they could see. Not a single one of the enemy had escaped.

25: King Jehoshaphat and his men went out to gather the plunder. They found vast amounts of equipment, clothing, and other valuables—more than they could carry. There was so much plunder that it took them three days just to collect it all!

26: On the fourth day they gathered in the Valley of Blessing, which got its name that day because the people praised and thanked the Lord there. It is still called the Valley of Blessing today.

2

Excruciating pain caused Pearl to call on Jesus

One night, I was babysitting a little six-year-old girl named Pearl. Pearl had a bad stomach ache. It was causing her excruciating pain, and she was screaming loudly. I had never seen her in such severe pain. We did not know if it was caused from something she drank or had eaten.

All I knew was that I could not think about what she might have ingested but rather what we could do about it. She was a big girl, but I held her tightly in my arms, rocking her back and forth. I felt helpless, and my heart was in deep agony seeing her that way. The agony of her pain held her for about fifteen minutes, which seemed much longer because I was trying to keep her calm.

I lay her down on the bed as she continued to scream and went into the kitchen to search for something that would relieve her of this horrendous pain. As I shuffled through the cabinets in the kitchen, I found a small bottle of medicine for the stomach for children. I rushed back to her, gently turned her over, lifted her head, and gave her the chewable tablet, hoping the pain would stop immediately. Then I sat on the side of the bed and lifted her back into my arms, rocking her with love.

Suddenly, a beautiful proclamation came out of her mouth so sincerely I will never forget it. She called on the name of Jesus! She said, "Jesus, help me."

Pearl spent a lot of time with us during the summers. Many times, we would have intimate talks about Jesus. Making it a time of importance, I would tell her sweetly that if she was ever in trouble, sick, sad, or needed help in school to always ask Jesus to help her. I never knew before if she had listened or absorbed it into her heart for use in times such as this.

Pearl's remembrance of crying, "Jesus, help me," brought the peace of Jesus' presence right at that moment. Now, she will forever know that she can count on Jesus for help because, at that moment, her pain stopped as I continued to rock her to sleep. Her desperate request was answered with love and relief from that excruciating pain. Pearl will always know that Jesus is her Helper, from personal experience and for life.

Psalm 121:2 (NLT): My help comes from the LORD, who made heaven and earth!

3

Assured seven-year-old orator

Pearl, who was only seven years old at the time, had the best memory I had witnessed that summer.

As I was getting Pearl settled in after her arrival at our home for the summer, I felt it was important to make her aware of our practice of making morning proclamations when we wake up and evening proclamations before we go to bed.

My husband and I had been listening to a pastor who, together with his wife, said proclamations before the pastor started teaching. They were scriptural proclamations to memorize and make a part of one's daily meditation. I typed out the proclamations so my husband and I could declare these truths daily. We wanted Pearl to be a part as well.

Before Pearl arrived, my husband and I had started saying our proclamations twice a day. My husband suggested that it would be good to memorize them, but we kept missing a word or two, sometimes a whole sentence, and we would burst out laughing at ourselves. We kept trying although we did not have them all memorized, and we were going into our third week.

When Pearl arrived, I gave her a copy of the proclamation. The next morning, we read it aloud together. I noticed Pearl said the proclamation with conviction, as if she already knew what she was saying applied to her. I believe this proclamation inspired her and moved her to claim it as her own.

I asked myself, "Does this seven-year-old girl understand God's will in this proclamation?" The proclamation was about two paragraphs long, double spaced.

The first day, we all read it together looking at the paper. The second day, we read it together looking at the paper, but then Pearl suggested we put the paper down and try reciting it from memory. We could not believe what we were hearing and seeing. Pearl put the paper down, gazed straight forward with squared shoulders, and spoke with assurance and confidence as an orator does when assured what they are saying is true and definite.

Pearl's outstanding memory and memorizing the proclamation on the second day dared us to look twice and know that Jesus had just performed a miraculous work in Pearl for His Glory.

Acts 8:6 (ONM): And the crowds paid attention to those things which were spoken by Philip. Of one mind in this, they listened and saw the signs which he was doing.

4

Start, then God will help you with the rest

I did not know how to start planning our wedding because we did not have much money to work with. I found myself at a standstill, at a loss, not knowing what to do.

I confided in a lady named Sarah who has been very sweet to me as long as I had known her. I felt assured I could reveal to her my concern about planning the wedding with very little money. With Sarah's calm disposition and experienced wisdom, she gazed ahead as if she had been in my shoes and knew exactly what to proclaim to me. With confident lips, her profound words spilled out the wisdom of God. Sarah declared, "Do whatever you can right now, and God will work out the rest."

Those words kindled my spirit into songs of joy, encouraging me to move forward toward planning. She advised me to start making a list of everything I needed for the wedding.

I heeded Sarah's instructions, immediately beginning to do what was possible for me to do at the time. As I was completing what I could do, unforeseen help suddenly started to spring in. I knew for sure that my Heavenly Father God had sent those who would help me with the rest of what needed to be done, as Sarah affirmed.

This wonderful journey I experienced has allowed me to graciously pass the baton to others who may think they have nothing to start with.

Sarah's lovingly encouragement, "Do whatever you can right now, and God will work out the rest," was one of the greatest prescriptions given to someone in need.

God definitely helped me with the rest. He took us to the finish line of a successful wedding to be remembered and showed us His goodness with the help of His child, Sarah.

James 2:22 (NLT): You see, his faith and his actions worked together. His actions made his faith complete.

5

Grace and Mercy told her what we needed

Wow! I was surprised when I opened the envelope! It was just what I needed! But who had told Ann what we needed?

We needed to make payments for our household responsibilities, and it did not seem like it was going to happen. Have you ever heard of having more month than money? Exactly! That is my point.

One of my husband's gifts has been his ability to call and arrange payments at later dates. There were times when representatives did not want to cooperate in allowing us to pay at a later date, but somehow my husband has always been able to persuade them of our need for assistance, which relieved us of being inconvenienced. It was the timing in the most needed situations that we were able to see the grace and mercy of God reaching out to us.

It was evident that Jesus put us on Ann's mind to assist us in our time of urgency. I believe when you trust in Jesus, He will speak to someone and put it on their heart to take action in helping someone else. I learned to never trust in the situation nor gaze at it. Jesus is our trusted Savior Who allows us to stand still and see His salvation for His glory. How sweet it is to witness the certainty of His love, and He continues to manifest His Word in our everyday existence. The Holy Spirit is all knowing, and He knows the end from the beginning.

As soon as I received Ann's gift, I called her immediately with great excitement and thanked her for it. I could feel the warmth of Ann's joy as I acclaimed my appreciation for her blessing us with a gift that came from Christ Jesus.

Thank you, Jesus, for Your faithfulness and for those who are faithful to your leading.

Hebrews 4:16 (NLT): So let us come boldly to the throne of our gracious God. There we will receive his mercy, and we will find grace to help us when we need it most.

6

Salvation rescued a friend

Where must I go? I had wondered to myself. I had been living in the same place all of my life. I had been at the same job since I graduated from high school. There seemed to be no forward movement in my life. I had starting to think I would be stuck there in my hometown forever.

Although Florida's beaches are exquisite and full of dazzling outdoor activities, I felt a need to see and explore something different. That did not impress upon me until I had been at my employment at the time for four years. Then something phenomenal happened.

As I arrived home and walked in the door, Lisa was on the phone with Patty who lives in Virginia. Lisa said, "Hey, Angela, Patty is on the phone. Do you want to speak to her?" I immediately said yes, not knowing what was about to happen.

Patty and I started chatting, and in the conversation, Patty said, "I wish I had people from home who would want to move here."

Yes, Patty was from my hometown and longed for someone she knew to move to Virginia where she lived. I could not believe what my ears were hearing. It was as if she had sung a delightful song I had been dreaming about. The door of opportunity had come dropping into my lap.

I started inquiring what Virginia offered that our hometown did not.

She told me about the opportunities and cultural things that Virginia offered and how exciting it was living there. Patty wanted a close friend to live there as well. From the way Patty explicated it, I knew at that moment I was willing to take a leap of faith and start my journey. I committed to Patty that my son and I would start making arrangements to move to Virginia.

One could not have imagined how excited I was about this exploration. We moved from Florida to Virginia because I wanted to experience something colossal and vast. I wanted to experience something that would make my eyes pop wide open and make me run around in awe. I'm from a small town in Florida, and our activities consisted of going to the beach or going to small clubs for excitement. I had never experienced living in a big city, so I decided to take a shot at it.

We moved, and there we started a new venture. As soon as my son and I arrived in Virginia, I started looking for employment. To my surprise, I was offered a very lucrative job working at a large corporation in McLean. Six years passed quickly, and although it seemed like my living status was increasing, I felt heavy hearted. As the time passed, it did not seem like joy was anywhere in sight. The future was looking bright, but my spiritual being was suffering.

I was actually going into my six year, moving up the ladder successfully, when suddenly my life and the way I was living flashed before my eyes. It was not pleasing to God nor myself, and I was beginning to feel an overwhelming feeling of guilt. I knew the reason.

I had met a man there, and he and I became very good friends. We became inseparable and were together all the time. Our relationship began to get serious, and we agreed to live together. We had lived together for about three years, and during that time, it did not seem like we were going toward the goal of getting married.

I started looking back over my life, and although it seemed like the relationship was going somewhere, it was not. I started to think more and more that I had made a mistake in considering living with a man I was not married to. This was not how I was raised. I knew what was right, and what I was doing was not right. It seemed the longer I stayed, the stronger the overwhelming feelings of guilt became.

One Sunday morning, I was feeling really low. Darkness was overshadowing me, and guilt was weighing me down. I decided to go to church, but I did not know where to go. I did not have a church home. At this point with the way I was feeling, I had to get to a church of God, so I started to drive. I kept on driving not knowing where I was going.

Then a song came on the radio that I had never heard before titled "What Shall I Do" by Tramaine Hawkins. The tears began to roll down my cheeks as she sang, "What shall I do? What step should I take? What move shall I make? Oh, Lord, what shall I do?"

By that time, I was crying uncontrollably and could not see where I was going. I pulled into a parking lot, continuing to cry, and I cried out to God, "What shall I do, dear God? What steps should I take?"

I did not realize I was sitting in a church parking lot because, when I parked, my head was down. When I finally looked up and saw where I was, joy filled my being! I got myself together and went inside. I felt like I was at home. Everyone welcomed me with open arms. I felt like all my burdens had been taken away.

That day, I dedicated my life to my Lord and Savior, Jesus Christ. Hallelujah! When I left church, I knew my life had been changed, and I had to change where I was living. I can gladly say that it was very easy because, when you have the love of Christ, you want to please Him in every way.

When I arrived home, I told the man I was living with that we could no longer live together, and he would have to leave because my life had changed. He respected my decision and packed up and left. His mother was very happy. She was a saved woman and told me never to stay with someone who does not want to marry you.

I had one more thing I had to do. I used to party with my friends, and that also was about to change. A particular friend was at my house and asked me to go to a club with her. I told her I would not be going to clubs anymore because my life had been changed. She could not understand why I did not want to go out anymore. I explained that I had accepted Jesus Christ as my Lord and Savior. She burst out crying and said she felt rejected. So I ask if she wanted to go to church with me the next Sunday. She hesitated at first, but then she said yes. We went to church the next Sunday, and she was very quiet. She had noticed the change in me and saw that I was very excited about being saved. Well, I kept going to church, but she did not go with me anymore, although we remained friends.

I felt like it was the end of my stay in Virginia, so I moved to Georgia. I had family there, and I wanted to be closer to home. The following year, that friend, with whom I used to party, came to visit me in Georgia.

A couple of years then passed and I learned that something miraculous had happened to her. She called to tell me she had started going to the same church I had gone to. She had received Jesus as her Lord and Savior. And this is the icing on the cake: she met someone at that same church, and he got down on one knee in front of the church and ask her to marry him. I cried on the phone, she and I screamed with joy thanking the Lord. Jesus Saves!

Psalm 28:6 (ONM): Blessed be the LORD because He has heard the sound of my supplications.

Colossians 1:13 (ONM): Who rescued us from the authority of the darkness and transferred us to the kingdom of the Son by His love ...

7

Jesus gave me breath to praise Him

When I was a child, I suffered terribly with asthma. I would get weak gasping for air, and my chest had agonizing pain. Many times, I was rushed to the emergency room. I would be petrified with fright, but I had to stay calm because my breathing would escalate to a fast pace making it worst.

I spent summers with my grandparents, and I would become very ill during my stay. No one could figure out why I would get the attacks when staying in Miami for the summer. I would also get sick at my own home and experience the same thing. How exhausting it was gasping for air and feeling like your breath is being taken away. I remember so vividly trying to catch my breath and feeling like I was fighting for my life.

These were long, lonely, dark times for me because it seemed like no one wanted to be near me. Many times, I would lie in bed suffering and asking myself if anyone really cared. There were no affirmations reassuring me that I would be okay. Maybe they were scared, too. As I write about this, those moments were very scary and real. At times, I did not think I would make it. It did not seem like the doctors knew in those days what they were doing, or at least I did not think they did.

I would lose so much weight in a week's time because I could not keep anything down. My great grandmother would give me soup, but I could not keep that down either. It would take at least a week to get my strength back. The chest pain from breathing so hard for such a long time was something I would not wish on anyone.

I hope I have given you my story of the real life sufferings I experienced in my childhood. Suffering from asthma in my childhood limited my playtime with other kids, not to mention missing weeks from school.

Although they seemed like very unhappy times, I now know Someone was always there inside of me breathing into my lungs and keeping me alive when I was gasping for air. Someone was always inside of me keeping me encouraged and keeping my dreams alive.

Looking back, I can see that Jesus was in the midst of all that suffering. I know and realize that every breath I take is for His glory. Jesus wanted me alive to tell everyone that He Saves!

I have been delivered and set free from asthma, but more importantly, I have been saved from sin. Now, with every breath I take, I will worship my Lord and Savior, Jesus Christ.

Psalm 150:6 (ESV): Let everything that has breath praise the LORD! Praise the LORD!

8

A divine secret message from the Holy Spirit

Back in the mid-1980s, my son and I moved from Florida to Virginia. My great grandmother had started visiting us every year. She was in her late 70s, still working, spunky, and fearless. It was phenomenal having someone of this nature help raise me.

When my great grandmother spoke, everyone listened because she spoke with wisdom and assertiveness. The tone of her voice commanded attention. Her words penetrated the mind and awakened the thoughts to remember always what she had spoken.

We were extremely excited she was flying to Virginia to visit us. She did not show one ounce of fear of flying alone. Her purpose was to get to where she was going. When she arrived, hugs and kisses were exchanged.

One thing I noticed about myself was that when my great grandmother was talking about something important, I would always sit at her feet and listen, conscientiously hanging onto every word she spoke. I always maintained a listening ear, feeling very grateful for her presence.

Often, I would hear a quiet voice in my spirit directing, "Take some professional pictures." Sadly, I did not heed the voice. My thoughts said, "I have time," or "I'll get it done on another occasion." Then after my great grandmother would fly back home, I would get an uneasy feeling that I should have done what was secretly messaged to me. I felt disgusted with myself that I did not put enough effort into getting those precious pictures taken.

Joyfully, when she visited the following year, my great grandmother was eighty years old. What a blessing to have an eighty-year-old senior visiting Virginia from Florida. During this visit, however, she showed signs that this would probably be her last trip.

When she arrived, there was something different about her, even in the way she talked. She did not mention anything about death, but her conversations were like she was at a final point and wanted to relieve everything that was on her mind.

We stayed up late at night talking about everything in life, things that she did not discuss with us growing up. Because of the drastic change in the way she was communicating and what she was communicating, I was very concerned. When she would be lying in bed asleep, I would check on her all during the night to make sure she was breathing. Fear of the end of my great grandmother's presence started to strike me with down-heartedness like a shooting arrow. No matter how hard I tried to get my mind distracted from it, her conversations would bring it back to mind.

Then the Holy Spirit spoke loudly and clearly to me, "You need to take pictures this time because she will not be back." This shook me up! I immediately made an appointment to have professional pictures taken. The photographer took some beautiful pictures of us together and of her alone.

My great grandmother left my home to go back to Florida and returned to work the same week. Can you believe at eighty years old she was still working? She had worked for several priests over a forty-year period.

One day when she was at work, one of the priests heard a fall on the bed. Not knowing what it was, the priest rushed into the bedroom to see what had happened. There, the priest saw my great grandmother lying on the bed not breathing. He quickly called an ambulance, but by the time they arrived, it was too late.

All of my great grandmother's visits were outstanding and awe-inspiring, but the last one will always be the most special time for me.

Not only did I receive her special love for me, but I received true love from the Holy Spirit who moved so faithfully in directing me to have a precious reminder of my dear, sweet great grandmother through those memorable pictures.

Hebrews 3:15 (GW): Scripture says, "If you hear God speak today, don't be stubborn. Don't be stubborn like those who rebelled."

9

You told her about "Me"

The time had come. I decided to leave Falls Church, Virginia, and move to Atlanta, Georgia. I was far away from home, and did not see family very often. Yes, it was time to move closer to home.

When I first moved away from home, moving away struck me as being a big deal. I moved far away from home because I felt like I was being independent. But years of maturing taught me something different. One can live down the street from relatives and still be independent. All I knew was that my heart longed to see my folks more often.

Although I longed to see my family more often, I was extremely sad leaving a few good friends behind, even though I would stay in contact with them as often as possible.

There was one special friend named Margaret whom I adored, and I would like to share this story. It is not easy, and I still cry like a little baby over what occurred. I loved Margaret deeply, and when I left Virginia, we kept in contact.

Margaret and I worked at a large corporation as executive secretaries. A man we both worked for who possessed a high ranking position was causing me problems. I will call him "Bob." Bob did not have a reason to have anything against me. It seemed he did not like that I was one of the Vice President's key persons, and the Vice President loved my work. I had some years under my belt of working at this corporation before Bob started working there. One day, Bob made some accusations about me to Margaret, my friend and coworker. Of course, Margaret communicated the accusations to me and was displeased with the remarks. She thought it was unprofessional to commit such an unethical disposition.

Margaret decided to go to the Vice President and tell him what was going on. She actually resigned, presenting a letter of why she was resigning. I had never had anyone stand up for me and defend me so strongly. She demonstrated fearlessness and exemplified a special friendship that will always be remembered.

My friend and I kept in touch. She knew my birthday and sent birthday cards every year. In the cards she would say, I'll be there to see you next year. I would call Margaret and thank her for the birthday card and tell her that I looked forward to her coming to Atlanta. We did not talk on the phone much, but when we did, we talked a long time.

When I called her one particular year, she was sick. I shared Christ Jesus with her, and she received Him as her Savior. I encouraged her and attested to her that Jesus is our Healer. Margaret agreed to the truth of Jesus' trusting Word. As she sighed with exhaustion throughout our conversation, she would assure me that she was getting better and would return to work soon.

Afterward, whenever I called Margaret, I would first call her office. I knew if she was at work, it meant she was recovering. Although I talked to her at home most of the time, Margaret would insist I call her at work. I believe she had high hopes of returning to work.

Margaret and I always managed to laugh about something in our conversations. It was delightful to hear her chuckle. But for some reason, when I would call her at work, they would say she was sick. Then I would call her at home, and she would tell me she was fine and that she would be at work soon. I would wait a while, call her job, thinking she would be there, to no avail. Margaret was not there. The receptionist said she did not know when my friend would be back. It never registered in my mind that something serious was happening. I did notice that she would never tell me what was wrong. Although she was a good friend of mine, I did not want to invade her privacy. We had conversations about a lot of things, but it was voluntarily.

I called her a few more times, thinking she would get better and call me. My life was very busy, and I failed to realize that so much time had passed.

One Sunday after church, my husband, my mother, and I wanted donuts, so we stopped by a donut shop. My husband and mother went in to get the donuts, and I stayed in the car. Margaret was on my mind, so I decided to call and surprise her. It was I who was surprised.

A man answered the phone. With excitement, I asked for Margaret. In His intimidating voice with woeful motives, he asked me who I was. I told him I was a good friend who used to live in Virginia.

Boom! My heart ripped to pieces hearing his reply! I burst out crying uncontrollably! I could not believe what I was hearing from the other end of the phone. He said Margaret had passed away two years ago. I was not aware it had been that long. I asked him what had happened. He abruptly made it clear he could not disclose information. I expressed my deep sympathy and hung up.

My husband and mother saw me sobbing and ran out to the car. They were completely in wonder as to why I was crying so unexpectedly. I could hardly talk because of the many emotions. I felt so guilty for not being there for her. I felt like a failure. I cried uncontrollably for weeks. For a long time afterward, every time I would think about her, it was as if I had just heard it all over again.

Then one day, the Holy Spirit spoke to me and took away all of my sadness and guilt. He said, "You told her about 'Me,' and that was the greatest goodbye." Hallelujah!

Romans 8:1 (ONM): There is therefore now no condemnation for those in Messiah Y'shua ...

10

Thank God, I forgave the handyman

Years ago, I had a Home Improvement Referral business. I was the liaison who interviewed contractors to see if they had all their credentials to qualify for doing jobs for customers.

One day, a particular contractor named Jay had an interview with me. He wanted me to send customers for his business. He repaired appliances for residential and commercial. This contractor considered himself a handyman. I set up an appointment with him and went to the designated place where our appointment was to be held.

I am always early for my appointments. As I sat there waiting, I noticed it was past the time we were to meet. I had called him the day before to confirm our appointment, and he said, yes, he would be there.

It was 15 minutes past the time we were to meet, so I called him. No answer. I waited about 45 minutes past the time we were supposed to meet. No call and no show. So I made a notation on the form I use to interview contractors and wrote "No call" and "No show" on the top of the form because I knew I would never use him. His behavior was a sign of irresponsibility. I took note that if Jay stood me up without calling, then he would certainly commit the same act toward customers.

Months went by, and I still did not hear a word from Jay after standing me up and exhausting my time. Then, with astonishment and shock, I heard the familiar voice on the phone. I instantly wanted to give him a piece of my mind. Thinking in disbelief, *the nerve he has to call back and ask for another opportunity!*

Jay spoke as if he was calling for the first time. I do not think he realized I remembered him. I said, "Aren't you the one who failed to show up for your appointment without even a phone call to say you couldn't make it?" He said he was sorry and that he would not do that again.

I could not trust Jay's apology. After all, he had not called to express his apology for a no show until I made him aware that I remembered him from the time before when we had an appointment. Then Jay started saying he was sorry over and over again, pleading his case to give him another fighting chance to show himself differently.

After listening to Jay's rant, I assured him that I had forgiven him, but I still did not want to use him because I have to think in terms of the customer's welfare. I am supposed to be sending contractors with credibility. Jay kept pleading with me to give him another chance. I hissed with a long hesitation ... he kept talking ... I still hesitated. Finally, I told him yes, I would give him another chance.

Hoping I had made the right decision, I sent Jay on a job, and the customer called me verbalizing his excellent work, stating that she would like for him to do some other projects around her house. My opinion of his needed skills went sky high, and he was well on its way to servicing customers for our company. Excitedly, Jay did about four jobs for us, and the comments on his great job performance were phenomenal.

While I was operating that business, I also had a part-time job. One day, while I was at my part-time job, I received an alarming message from Jay's wife asking me to call. She was crying uncontrollably. I quickly returned the call, and what I heard was startling and unbelievable. My whole being shifted to a traumatic disposition not understanding what was going on. I had just communicated with Jay the day before. She said her husband was in the hospital and that he was diagnosed with a fast-spreading stomach cancer, and they had given him two weeks to live.

The news was an absolute bombshell and a turning point for all those who knew him. I did not know what to do or say at the time. I was trying to comprehend whether or not this was actually true. After a moment of hearing Jay's wife explaining and crying about this shattering condition, I broke out of my internal disturbance and began to console and encourage her with the Word of God. He is our Peace.

When she seemed to calm down, I gently asked her where he was and told her that my husband and I would visit him in the hospital.

I could not concentrate on my job for the rest of the day, constantly hearing his wife's words of despair echoing in my mind. That evening, I told my husband about it, and we took our Bibles and other encouraging books and went to visit Jay.

When my husband and I arrived at the hospital, we prayed with Jay and asked him if he had repented and accepted the Lord Jesus Christ as his personal Savior? He said no. We asked him if he wanted to, and he said yes. My husband and I had Jay to repeat after us as we led him to repentance and a commitment to living his life in Christ. We talked about Jesus, what He had done for him on the Cross, and about Jesus' faithfulness. Our conversation was all about Christ Jesus and His goodness.

We spent a lot of time on the phone with Jay and his wife, and she also accepted the Lord Jesus as her Savior. I remember when Jay said that whether he lived or died, he was happy he had Jesus and that he had peace. Jay passed, but he has a life with Christ Jesus!

What was the most moving and life-changing experience for me was that I had forgiven Jay, not knowing what was going to happen in the future. Forgiveness is absolutely freeing because Jesus is our perfect example of it! Praise the Living Jesus!

Acts 8:35 (NLT): So beginning with this same Scripture, Philip told him the Good News about Jesus.

Mark 11:25 (NIV): "And when you stand praying, if you hold anything against anyone, forgive them, so that your Father in heaven may forgive you your sins."

11

Jesus excellently sustains

No one would have guessed in a million years that my husband would be interviewed and hired the same day. Yes, he was hired on the spot.

We were in a tight and pressing situation financially. My husband decided to ask Joe at the church we were attending if he knew of any job openings. Joe told my husband about interviews that would be held at a particular hotel for specific jobs.

The day before interviews were supposed to be held, my husband called the hotel to confirm. Well, that was a smart move because they told my husband it had been cancelled, but another company would be there doing interviews and hiring on the spot.

Of course, my husband did not know all of the details until arriving at the location, but the night before, he ask me if I wanted to go and apply since I was out of work as well. I responded yes, I would like to see what the job was all about.

We arose early in the morning and affirmed on our way that we would come back with jobs. When we arrived, to our amazement, people were in long lines backed out toward the main lobby area. We knew many people were out of work, but there was something distinctive about this setting.

The company had everyone to read over general information about the company. We discovered it was an oil company in another state. We thought the oil company must be setting up a station in Atlanta. So, with excitement, we moved right along wanting to know more information.

In the next step, the oil company encouraged us to view a video explaining the company's work advantages and dangers. After the video ended, we wondered if people would be discouraged because of the various risks to be considered when working for this oil company.

Many people stayed, and many walked out. Of course, as I was viewing the video, I knew my vote was out the window.

What took everyone by surprise was that after the video was over, they had to make a decision right then whether or not they would take the position. They were doing drug tests on the spot. Some passed, some did not.

As my husband was holding his paper, we looked at each other, and he asked me those unexpected words, "Honey, should I agree to this?" I shook my head in disbelief, not knowing what our answer should be. Part of me felt like I would be sending my husband out to war, and the other part was asking if this was from God.

We had no money coming in at all. We did not want to be foolish and not take it when an opportunity had been dropped in our laps and then still be asking the Lord for work.

Remembering that His sovereign Word is brought to us when we need it is comforting. Jesus brought this work to us to sustain us. And in the midst of all its dangers, He would protect us. With this truth in mind, we agreed that my husband would accept the offer in Texas.

Although my husband would be away from me, we were so grateful for how the Lord Jesus worked everything out at the last moment. His ways are definitely higher than our ways, and His thoughts are higher than our thoughts. The way Jesus rescued us was un-thought of. It was effortless victory! It was simply amazing! Jesus' visibility and His wondrous works are for the world to see that He is God alone.

That job paid so well that when we would go to the doctor, they treated us like royalty because of the type of insurance we had. Their expressions were like WOW. They were in disbelief that we had insurance like that. God blessed us so much. We were able to go to the doctor, the dentist, and the eye doctor, something we had been unable to do before. I was able to get special contacts that were required by my eye doctors. In the past, I had not been able to afford them, but Jesus could! Hallelujah!

Psalm 54:4 (NASB): Behold, God is my helper; The Lord is the sustainer of my soul.

12

I saw God in Utah

In my early twenties, I used to collect magazines of places I wanted to visit, plenty of them. I would gaze at the pictures and imagine I was there enjoying the scenery and surroundings. Two of my favorite places I wanted to venture out to were Colorado and Alaska. I have had memorable experiences enjoying different beaches but never the mountains. Seeing the grandeur of the mountains ranges with their alluring landscapes stretching magnificently across the magazines' pages would cause me to blurt out, "Aww, nice." It immediately put my mind at ease as I paused to relish the stunning essence made by our Creator God.

I was fascinated by how high and towering the mountain were. I am a Florida girl, born and raised, and I have always admired the soft, and sometimes rough, waves pushing back and forth on the shore with a constant breeze blowing against your face. When I'm at the beach, the scenery puts me in an atmosphere of the presence of the Lord. The water flowing back and forth showing off the white foaming waves is absolutely exquisite. When it is time to leave the beach, it is as if all your negative thoughts have rolled off the shore into the great deep waters never to return again.

Although, I am captivated by dazzling beaches, there was something inside of me that wanted to see the huge mountains that tower toward the sky as if touching it.

I had it settled in my mind that the only way I would ever be able to see the huge, stunning mountains was to capture them on the computer or in magazines, until one unforgettable day when God decided to let me see Him in a way I have never before seen Him.

My husband, Elliott, applied for a position to sell blender machines and was interviewed on Skype. Peter, the interviewer, was quite impressed with my husband's character and felt he would do well with the company. When Peter asked my husband if he was married, Elliott said yes and then, of course, took the liberty of convincing Peter that we work closely in other ventures. Peter asked Elliott if I would like to do the business with him. Elliott called out to me from the other room asking if I would like to join him in this new endeavor. I excitedly responded with an assured "Yes!"

Elliott continued with the interview and was hired. After he accepted the offer, Peter said he would be sending two tickets for us to be flown to Utah. My mouth flew open in amazement! I could not believe what I was hearing. God made the way for us to see those towering mountains I had always longed to see. My heart was filled with gratitude and thankfulness to the Lord Jesus for making the way for me to see the mountains I have gazed at in magazines and on the computer.

Peter assured us that he would be setting a date for us to fly to Utah for training. When we hung up the phone, I was jumping up and down, overjoyed like a little kid in an ice cream store who had just been told to pick anything he wanted.

About three to four weeks later, Peter booked our tickets to Utah for a week. In my mind, I was thinking, "Lord, is this really happening? Are we going to Utah?" We were on the plane headed to Utah. I was trying to stay relaxed, but my body was elated with unimaginable joy. My thoughts were racing with questions about the unknown.

To relieve all of this, I meditated on the Word of God. Then His peace overtook me, carrying away all of my anxiousness. It was at that moment that God's presence consumed me with patience, and my mind centered on Him, welcoming His magnificence.

Time passed, and then we heard the unthinkable announcement that we would be landing soon. I looked out the window, although my husband was sitting by the window. As we were going down, breaking through the clouds, I saw the most magnificent sight I had ever seen—huge, breathtaking mountains. This was certainly better than looking at a magazine or the internet.

When we arrived, it was nearly dark. We retrieved our suitcases and waited for our driver to take us to the hotel, which was a forty-minute drive. By that time, I was tired and wanted to get some rest for the next day. My husband and I had to be in the lobby by 8:00 AM for the shuttle to pick us up for training.

The next morning, I got up extra early to go outside the hotel to take pictures, and I could not believe what I was seeing. Huge mountains, as high as the sky, surrounded Salt Lake City.

As I was staring at the mountains, tears began streaming down my cheeks. I fell down on my knees, put my camera down, and worshipped the Lord, telling Him of His goodness, His awesomeness, His beauty, and His faithfulness. I was overwhelmed with the presence of God and saw Him in a way I had never before seen Him. I saw another part of the world that God had formed with His Word. I thanked Him for giving me the desire of my heart.

Jesus allowed me to see the loveliness that He had formed so beautifully upon the earth. Hallelujah!

Hebrews 1:10 (ONM): And, "You, Lord, laid the foundation of the earth from the beginning, and the heavens are the works of Your hands …"

13

Gladly obeyed Holy Spirit in Arkansas

My husband and I were doing demonstrations marketing a blender in Little Rock, Arkansas. We were there for almost two weeks and worked fourteen long hours per day. Since we knew someone close to us there, we thought we would be able to socialize with them during our down time. Unfortunately, most of our down time was after 10:00 PM. But as tired as we were, we still made time for Valerie.

We spent a few nights with Valerie, enjoying her company and being much appreciative for offering her home for us to get some rest. One of the nights we lodged over at Valerie's house, my husband fell asleep, and Valerie and I continued enjoying each another's company.

As Valerie and I were sharing, she began to disclose what she had been experiencing with her health. If she had not reached out, I would not have known because she looked great. I did not know why she had reached out to me, but this I did know: there was the Holy Spirit inside of me Who wanted to reach out and touch Valerie with God's assured Word of healing her right at that moment.

Valerie continued to express that she had been having problems with her eyes and suffering terribly in different parts of her body. The intensity of God's grace and His mercy began to boil in me with compassion. Valerie continued, saying that at one time it was very hard for her to walk because there was so much pain in her feet. Valerie was experiencing discomfort with her eyes, and they would get red and swell. She went to the doctor, and they could not figure out what was going on in her body.

After Valerie released her worries and discomforts, I boldly assured her that Jesus had already taken away all of her sicknesses and diseases, if she believed He did.

It was very late, and we both had to prepare for bed because we all had to get up early in the morning. We departed to our rooms, and I got down on my knees and started to pray for her with deep compassion and concern. My heart cried out to the Lord Jesus for her because she lives alone and desperately needed His help. Suddenly, the Holy Spirit said, "Go and touch her heels in the Name of Jesus."

Hesitation was my natural response, and I thought to myself, *Will she believe me; will she do it?* I definitely believed and wanted to do the command of the Holy Spirit. The Holy Spirit said, "Do it NOW!"

I got up immediately and knocked on Valerie's door, brazenly stating, "The Holy Spirit told me to touch your heels in the Name of Jesus." She said, "I'm good, but if you want to, you can." I told her I wanted to be obedient to the Holy Spirit and that it was up to her. She responded that it was okay.

I touched both of her heels in Jesus' name, and then we embraced one another. She thanked me, and I thanked God for her healing. I reminded her that Jesus had already taken care of her healing at the Cross when He shed His blood and died for us. She understood. She went back to her room, and I went to my sleeping quarters.

I was honored to obey the commands of the Holy Spirit with gladness. Witnessing walking by faith and not by sight, the way Christ Jesus commands us to live, we are offering our bodies as a living sacrifice, holy and acceptable in His sight.

The next evening, I received a phone call from Valerie proclaiming that her heels were better, and her eyes were completely clear and had not been that clear in a long time. She said they felt so much better and thanked me. I responded that she should thank Christ Jesus. He did it over two thousand years ago. I advised her to keep thanking Jesus for her healing. After hanging up from Valerie, I stretched out my hands to God and proclaimed, "To God be the Glory. Thank You, Jesus. Hallelujah!"

Acts 4:30 (NLT): "Stretch out your hand with healing power; may miraculous signs and wonders be done through the name of your holy servant Jesus."

14

Jesus keeps an eye on His sheep

My husband and I had just arrived home from attending Wednesday night service for the first time at this particular church. After arriving home, we went about our usual routine before going to bed.

Several hours passed, and I decided to go into the kitchen to get a snack when, suddenly, I started to have pains around my navel area. I challenged my memory bank to remember what I had done or eaten before going to church. I could not think of anything that would have caused the discomfort I felt.

I went on to the kitchen to prepare a drink of some cayenne and warm water to relieve the pain. But as I reached for the cayenne, the Holy Spirit bid me to STOP! The Holy Spirit commanded that if I pray in the name of Jesus, and I would be healed RIGHT NOW! I was convinced this was the Holy Spirit guiding me to be delivered in the name of Jesus. Therefore, with no hesitation, but with assured faith, I obeyed the Holy Spirit and affirmed in the name of Jesus that I am healed because the blood of Jesus healed me over two thousand years ago.

After I declared my healing in the name of Jesus, the pain stopped instantly. Heeding the instructions of the Holy Spirit is certainly gratifying. I have not had any pains in my navel area since then. Jesus' faithfulness and love always remind us of His goodness and how He keeps an eye on His sheep. Jesus' wondrous works keep us aware that He is always present. All we have to do is hearken to His guidance, and we will see Him in ACTION! Hallelujah!

Hebrews 3:7-8 (ESV): Therefore, as the Holy Spirit says, "Today, if you hear his voice, do not harden your hearts as in the rebellion, on the day of testing in the wilderness ..."

15

A sword raised for surgery

What I'm sharing here is not easy to express without shedding tears of joy. I will push through all of what I experienced during this particular season.

My husband, Elliott, came home early from work one afternoon. He was greatly concerned because he had shortness of breath and his heart was beating very hard.

As he was describing the symptoms, he asked if I would listen to his heart, and without a doubt, it was beating fast and strong, as if someone was banging a drum. We made a quick decision that he should be rushed to the emergency room.

When we arrived at the hospital, they immediately admitted him. They hooked him up to machines for testing. After hours of testing, they could not find anything wrong. They gave him a stress test and still could not find anything.

Although we were glad they could not find anything, we knew there was something going on in his body and did not feel comfortable returning home without knowing what it was.

They were about to release him but decided to give him one final test to see if they would come up with anything. Not surprisingly, they detected a 90% blockage in his heart. They were close to releasing my husband to go home with a 90% blockage in his heart! They asked him if he had ever had a heart attack, and he responded never. They were astonished because of the ninety percent blockage.

Urgently, they rushed Elliott via ambulance from the hospital he was in to another hospital for surgery. I had to quickly pack up our things from the hospital we were in and rush to get to the hospital where his surgery would be performed.

As I was driving to the other hospital, I felt Jesus upholding me with His presence and comforting me with His great peace. He was assuring me that my husband would be absolutely made whole, that He would be with my husband and the doctors.

With all of my being, I trusted the Lord, and I was determined that fear was not going to take over Jesus' guaranteed truth that was whispered in my being. From there, Jesus' Word was my sword and anchor blocking all the lies of fear. I broke down and cried and cried, but through my tears, I raised up the Sword of His Word, and declared it, and I raised my voice in worship to Jesus, which kept peace present.

I saw part of my husband's surgery, and it looked as if he was fighting for his life. In the midst of this surgery, I saw my Savior, Jesus Christ, at work keeping my husband alive. I witnessed the salvation of Jesus in action as He miraculously accomplished His Word. Suddenly, it became evident that our Jesus had gone ahead of us and had already won the battle for us. Hallelujah! Jesus is our Deliverer!

Exodus 14:14 **(GW)**: "… The LORD is fighting for you! So be still!"

Ephesians 6:17 **(NLT)**: Put on salvation as your helmet, and take the sword of the Spirit, which is the word of God.

16

A love letter to Great-Grandmother

One evening as I was sitting, my great grandmother, Dora, was heavily on my mind. I began to think about how much I deeply love and adore her. I reminisced about my childhood endeavors and the precious time my great-grandmother Dora gave, wanting nothing in return. My heart was filled with joy.

I suddenly felt an urge, like fire in my belly, to express all of my feelings of love in a letter to be given personally to this adored lady. At the time, she was 78 years young, strong as an ox, and still working six days a week.

It was 1985, and as I wrote, it was as if the letter had already been written in my heart. The words were flowing like soft waves rolling out to the sea. I began with making it known that I loved her. I thanked her for loving me and for tending to me when I suffered from asthma attacks as a child.

I thanked her for all of the times I would pop the question, "Can you make me some flour bread?" This flour bread was freshly cooked on top of the stove, and with no hesitation, she would always agree with no complaining, no matter how tired she was from working long, 12-hour days. I passionately commended her as being the best great-grandmother in the world.

I am grateful for the blessed time she spent visiting my son and me in Virginia. My love letter went on and on with thanksgiving as I emptied myself making her aware of how she has always been an important person to me and how she continued to bring unspeakable joy into my life.

This love letter could have gone on and on, but I had to come to a close. The letter was concluded and mailed, to my great grandmother's surprise. When she received it and read it, she was overwhelmed by what she read. She took the letter to the church she attended to share it with the minister. The minister was so touched with what my great-grandmother shared that he wanted to share it with the congregation. So the minister read it out loud to the congregation and preached on it. The minister acclaimed, this is how a child should let their mothers, grandmothers and love ones know how much they love them while they are alive because you do not know how long they may be on this earth. My great-grandmother was 78 at this time. After the minister finished, my great-grandmother said she was so full of joy and as she was sharing it with me so was I.

My great grandmother passed at exactly 80 years old, and it gave me great pleasure to have followed my heart consciously and intentionally verbalizing an expressed love for her while she was alive.

The most unusual thing happened at her funeral. I had expected that I would take her death really hard when that day arrived and that I would shed many tears. However, when that day came, only a few drops fell. I realized the peace of God was with me. Then I realized that I was the one truly blessed by her life, and it had been expressed in her actions throughout my life. Thank you, Jesus, for my great-grandmother's life.

---

1 Peter 1:22 (NIV): Now that you have purified yourselves by obeying the truth so that you have sincere love for each other, love one another deeply, from the heart.

17

Increased worship received manifested plans

The Holy Spirit spoke to me on New Year's Eve of 2011 to increase my worship. Holy Spirit said that when I increase my worship and make my life a life of worship to Him, I would see His manifested plans for me for the rest of my life.

Upon receiving this revelation from the Spirit of the Lord, He heard my cry. There is nothing more unfavorable than living this life here on earth without the plans of Jesus. Many times, I felt as if I was lost in a desert trying to find the plans Jesus had for me. My heart longed to be fully committed to Jesus and to please Him with my whole being until He returns. I was passionate about seeking the plans Jesus had for me because I no longer wanted to live my life in vain.

Many times in my life I have done the planning, and without admitting to it, there was an emptiness residing in me most of the time. I knew that God's plan alone would fill every empty place in me.

Before crying out to the Lord, I never knew that worship and thankfulness would bring out God's plans and directions. The Holy Spirit explained that I had a lot to worship the Lord Jesus for and that my eyes would be open to God's plan.

Interestingly, the guest speaker at the church we were visiting for New Year's Eve has an extreme passion for influencing others to worship our Lord and Savior, Jesus Christ. I did not know this until after the service when I was looking at the book table. I could not believe that God had sent someone with a passion for what God wanted me to do. This was a straight command from the Holy Spirit, and I knew this was the answer from God for my life.

I shared with the guest pastor that the Holy Spirit had told me to increasing my worship. She was so excited about what I told her. The books and newsletter she brought were all about worship, just what the Holy Spirit said I needed. Obediently, I bought the books and have been greatly blessed by them.

My worship has increased, and I am in the presence of the Lord Jesus more than ever before. His directions are very clear, with understanding. The most exciting experience about it all, Jesus has given me boldness through my worship to reach those who are lost. Hallelujah!

John 4:23 (ESV): But the hour is coming, and is now here, when the true worshipers will worship the Father in spirit and truth, for the Father is seeking such people to worship him.

Psalm 119:125 (NASB): I am your servant; give me understanding, that I may know Your testimonies.

18

I found a loving dad in a father-in-law

Years ago, God brought a man into my life, and I had no clue I would be experiencing him as a father.

I grew up without a father being in the home, but I met my biological father, or acknowledged him as being my father, between the ages of seven and eight years old. All I remember is being picked up and taken to his house.

My father and grandfather owned a BP station on the beach, and I remember my sisters and I were many times taken to the BP station to see them. How exciting it was to walk down the street and see the waves rolling back and forth on the shore. Sometimes our father would take us to the beach to play for a while.

I did not consider that my father and I had a close relationship, but I remember being so happy that he was my dad. I was well informed of some of his achievements, and he seemed to be well known among our neighboring cities. Although I did not have a close relationship with him, I felt I was blessed to have a father who was the first Black man to have owned a BP station on Cocoa Beach in the 1970s.

My father was also a musician and had a black belt in Karate. He was very popular around town. I was very pleased with his accomplishments but never experienced a father-daughter relationship.

What was mysterious about my feelings for my father is that although I did not know him, I loved him deeply. As a child you cannot seem to figure out how the story goes and how it should end.

My father died when I was young. Therefore, an emptiness and a misunderstanding of why I did not experience a father's love is what I was left with for an ending story.

My father-in-law moved from Arkansas to Georgia in 2008 to live with my husband and me. I did not know that I was in for one of the best father-in-law/daughter-in-law experiences of my life.

After he arrived, I felt like a little girl being loved by a father, something I had never experienced in my life. It was as if I had gone back in time to fill all the gaps of what I had missed as a small child with her father. I even called him "Dad," which felt natural because of the way my father-in-law expressed his love toward me. When he spoke, I felt like a little girl sitting "crisscross applesauce" at his feet listening to his life stories as he shared with us at our famous meeting place at the kitchen table.

Many times, all three of us would be in the kitchen cooking up something to eat. Someone might be doing the cutting, the other rinsing off something, and the other cooking. What a great team we made making meals prepared with love.

My father-in-law, my husband, and I met at the kitchen table faithfully almost every day for breakfast, lunch, and dinner. We did not just eat and leave the kitchen table. Meaningful conversations took place at the kitchen table. Hearty laughs and serious and adventurous conversations captured our interest.

His lifetime experiences and the way he explained them were always intriguing. The highlight of every day was at our kitchen table. Breakfast, lunch, and dinner Dad was telling us his experiences that were believable and sometimes far-fetched. Either way, we enjoyed him sharing his lifetime active involvements, keeping us occupied with laughter and wows.

Helen, one of my husband's younger sisters, and our grandbaby Pearl came to spend time with us for the summer. My husband and Helen signed up to be in a talent/fashion show at a neighboring mall, and we had a grand and exciting time seeing them perform down the runway. My father-in-law got a kick out of seeing his son and daughter do their creative performances. Every Saturday we would all pile up in Dad's utility vehicle and go to the mall to see them strut their talent. What fun we had applauding and jumping up and down with enthusiasm.

When I roll back the camera of my thoughts, there was never a dull moment in our togetherness. We even went as far as being extras in a well-known movie.

My father-in-law always wanted to be a part of our ventures, which led us to doing almost everything inseparably.

One of our fun dinner table experiences was when Dad told us about when he and some friends were sitting on some wood eating their lunch when they noticed that the wood moved a little. They did not think anything of it, so they kept eating. This time the wood moved a little bit more, and they all took off running for dear life. The most hilarious part about this story was that he was running so fast his heels were hitting the back of his head. We laughed so hard we were about to fall out of our chairs.

When we think about it now, we break out with laughter because Dad was serious about what he was saying, and you dared not think it was not so.

There were so many of my father-in-law's stories that captivated our attention and brought us closer and closer as a family. Then something struck that changed our lives. How quickly something can change the tides from joy to downheartedness.

The overwhelming news that was communicated to us by the doctor regarding my father-in-law was inconceivable and beyond belief. This man who was like a dad to me became very ill, and his health started going down rapidly. The doctor told the family that Dad had only weeks to live.

I raced out of the room, bursting into uncontrollable tears, devastated about what I had just heard. I could not process this. It did not make sense. I asked myself if this was really happening.

I was standing outside of Dad's hospital room door crying and feeling trapped in this state of mourning. I was trying to get myself together to go back into the room to show support for my inlaws, but the tears would not stop. I went to the nearest restroom, and the tears were continuing to fall like hard rain drops. I called on the name of Jesus saying, "Jesus, help us!" I took a couple of deep breaths, and although the tears would not stop flowing, I went back into the room.

When I entered Dad's hospital room, I suddenly felt that what God had given me, which was a dad and a friend I deeply loved for the first time in my life, was being taken away. I was losing the father-daughter relationship that I cherished. Dad always called me daughter, and I always called him dad from the first time we met.

The situation was difficult for me to grasp as a reality. At that moment, I knew I had to seek Jesus for comfort and peace. I quieted myself to listen to the Spirit of the Lord, and through being still, Jesus consoled me with the presence of His love.

Jesus had made sure that I had an example and an understanding of a father who exemplified unconditional love. And although it was short lived, it gave me great joy to know Jesus' love is never short lived but everlasting. Jesus wiped away all my tears with His unconditional love.

It's beyond our thoughts when God brings the most wonderful experiences in our lives so we can see Him filling every void that we may or may not acknowledge in our lives. Jesus' love grips and satisfies us with the testaments of His love.

Jesus definitely uses other people to complete every one of His purposes here on earth. I thank God for using Henry Simpson to show me a dad's love here on earth that will always be remembered. And I thank You, Jesus, for giving me this experience you knew about in advance to bring Glory to Your Name and peace to my heart.

---

2 John 1:3 (NLT): Grace, mercy, and peace, which come from God the Father and from Jesus Christ—the Son of the Father—will continue to be with us who live in truth and love.

19

Stand at attention!
Bold message showed me who I am

Boldness is always what I wanted. Not just boldness but boldness in proclaiming the Gospel of Jesus Christ. My spirit was crying out for boldness to reach those who are lost like I once was. This was an urgency in my heart. I asked the Lord Jesus for boldness in Him.

One day, the Holy Spirit quietly said, "If you want to be bold, listen to bold messages." I understood what the Lord was saying. I just did not know how it was going to be done.

My husband and I had been listening to a particular preacher on YouTube for about a year, and we were greatly blessed by how the Lord used him to bring others into the Kingdom of God.

One particular night after listening to this preacher, my husband gently turned toward me and asked if I wanted to listen to Reinhard Bonnke. I had heard of Reinhard Bonnke but had never heard him preach, so I said yes.

When I look back at how kindly I said yes, I know the Holy Spirit was in it because the teaching I was getting was greatly blessing me at the time, and there was tremendous growth as a result. I had no clue God was about to pour out that I needed to possess boldness for His Kingdom.

When my husband pulled up Reinhard Bonnke on YouTube, I was lying down. But when I heard his voice and the boldness of his preaching,

I raised up as if something gripped my very being. Instantly, and without a doubt, I knew Reinhard Bonnke was the one the Holy Spirit was using to show me a bold believer preaching the gospel of Jesus Christ.

I believe the reason my spirit gravitated to this preaching is that it was solely about souls being saved, nothing more and nothing less. The entire message was about the urgency of souls being saved and boldly coming to Christ NOW! I had never heard such bold teaching on salvation, with the intent that Jesus can show up right now, so be ready.

From that time on, I was listening to Reinhard Bonnke every day from the time I woke up to the time I went to bed. I felt like my spirit was in desperate need of this bold teaching. It was not just a bold message, it was a strong message of hope and the promised love of Jesus Christ.

When listening to this kind of bold teaching, you were sure you did not want to live a life without Jesus. You were persuaded that with repentance came a Savior who would embrace, protect, and lovingly make you His very own for eternity.

The bold truth of God's Word taught through Reinhard Bonnke made you want to run out into the street and yell aloud, "Repent, every one of you, for Jesus is near. Salvation has been paid for by Jesus' blood." My spirit could not get enough of the Good News being preached in truth and with boldness.

Reinhard Bonnke's passion for reaching the lost, and the way he lives for Christ Jesus, encourages believers to say, "Here am I, Lord, send me," and then to go out there and do it.

When you believe what Jesus has done for you through His shed blood stopping sin and death in your life to live a righteous life with Him, it is a great honor. You are so convinced, you do not want to live any other life but with Him. You become consumed with Jesus' presence, believing His instructions are for our good and that anything else is in vain.

When the Holy Spirit is proclaiming the Good News through us, it captures and grips the hearts of the lost and fills their hearts with the love of Jesus. And when they truly know and understand what Jesus has done for them, they will never want to turn back to living a life of opposition toward God.

At times, we are shown through others Who it is that exists in us. Christ exists in them to encourage us to move forward with what God has called us to do.

I believe this is what happened to me when my husband introduced me to the teaching of Reinhart Bonnke. He caused me to stand straight up like a soldier in the army of God and reminded me of who I am in Him and what I'm supposed to be doing. After all, we are one body of Christ Jesus.

For sure, I knew this is how I wanted to live my life. I wanted to reach as many people as I can, while I still have breath. Proclaiming the "Good News of Jesus Christ" is a priority and a desire, and this is how I want to live, move, and have my being in Jesus.

To proclaim the Good News of Jesus Christ for souls to be saved is urgent and necessary. We must all make this a priority, for the time is near and boldness is imperative. The light of Jesus is the Good News preached to the lost with confidence and boldness.

Let us take action in the Body of Christ Jesus and snatch them out of the fire as Christ did for us. Let us not allow timidity to withhold our tongues from proclaiming the gospel of Jesus Christ, for it is our right and our instruction from God. We will show love to another as an example

Now, I can truly say I have boldness and a passion through Christ Jesus for the lost, to bring them to Him because Jesus SAVES! Hallelujah!

Acts 4:13 (ONM): And when they saw the boldness of Peter and John and understood that they were unlearned and unskilled men, they were astonished and recognized them, because they had been with Y'shua.

20

The beginning of creation brought worship and true love

I never knew love like this until I had an understanding of worship. I went back to the beginning of Genesis and read how that God had created everything with His Word. Although I have read this before, this time I gained a greater understanding through the Holy Spirit. I began to understand more and more Who God is. He is Power and Authority, and it is shown all from His Spoken Word.

The action of God's Word created the earth in perfect form. I began to meditate deeply on God's Sovereignty and the beauty of His Works. As I pressed in deeper into God's presence by meditatively observing His magnificence from the beginning of creation, this drew me to a heartfelt worship.

Going back to the beginning also revealed a clear picture of who I am in Christ Jesus and how I was created to worship the One Who created me for Himself.

Understanding the beginning from Genesis has drawn me closer to Jesus Christ than ever before, knowing that it has always been an underlying purpose of our existence to worship the King of kings and Lord of lords.

As I continued to meditate on God's wonderful works, I found myself embracing His authority upon the earth, and His position gave more understanding and meaning than ever before. At that moment, I felt a deep desire to know Him in His fullness.

When I read Genesis, I began to see God's visibility in everything in the earth, and that was exciting. God's presence was always there as I took notice of what God did when He spoke the Heavens and the Earth into existence. God's power and authority raised awareness in me that He still commands things out of nothingness.

I am a witness of Jesus bringing victory out of nothingness in my life. My relationship with Jesus and being in His presence has sharpened my awareness of His sovereignty. These magnificent works of His have brought me understanding of His love and how He shares love all over the world that His children might see Him.

I went back to the beginning because I needed a refresher course and a reminder of the God I worship. Going back to the beginning gave me a full picture and an assurance of God's supreme and incomparable position. He is Majesty, He is Just, He is Honorable, He is Power, He is Authority, and He is the Beginning and End.

NOW when I worship my Lord and Savior, I can truly say I know Him. God's glory is always made visible to those who know Him and diligently seek Him. Worship is all about knowing Him and knowing who you are in Him. His Spirit and Truth live on the inside of us and are expressed in deep love by His miraculous works!

Genesis 1:31 (ONM): And God saw everything that He had made and, behold, it was very good. And there was evening and there was morning, the sixth day.

21

God gave me great news for my future

January 13, 2013, at 1:40 PM, my husband, Elliott, presented a question out of nowhere that I would normally stumble over. The question was, "Do you know God's plan for your life?" Without hesitation, I emphatically responded with a confident "yes."

For the first time, there was no doubt in my conscious mind of the plans the Lord had for me to bring glory to His Name. After my husband heard my assured response, he cross examined me, "Are you sure?" I gazed into his eyes with absolute certainty and said, "Yes, I know God's plan for me!"

God's Word has been very clear and understandable regarding His plan for me. It became clear when I made a decision that I would trust Jesus and continually seek His direction. I would be conscious not to lean to my own understanding that opposes His direction.

Going my own way for many years led me to an unfruitful result. At times, when I tried to plan ahead, the Holy Spirit stopped me and said, "Do not go ahead of Me. I will stay ahead of you. This way your steps are assured all the way to the end." Therefore, I would rather follow the One Who created me and knows exactly what glorifies Him.

God's instruction to me included being single minded and having a bullseye about His perfect plan for me. I decided I wanted to follow God's plan that will never be in vain and will always honor Him.

I am aware that my Savior's ways are higher than mine and His thoughts are higher than mine. Therefore, I desire to live, move, and have my being in Jesus' ways and His thoughts. I absolutely believe God's ways are effective and will bring those that are lost to His Kingdom.

His action plan for me is to reach those that are lost and bring them to salvation. This is "GREAT NEWS" for my future plans from Christ Jesus. Jesus is leading me every step of the way by the Fire of His Word. Jesus is always letting me know that His presence is with me daily. Hallelujah!

Jeremiah 29:11 (ESV): For I know the plans I have for you, declares the LORD, plans for welfare and not for evil, to give you a future and a hope.

22

A Christmas blessing from our grandbaby, Elizabeth

My husband and I took a trip to Florida to visit our grandbabies the weekend of Christmas 2012. Our grandbabies are young, and I make it a point to see them on a regular basis to maintain our relationship. When I was a child, we had visits every summer with my grandparents as far back as I can remember. Therefore, having a relationship with our grandbabies is very important to me.

On this particular Christmas day, something very special happened. My husband and I bought our youngest grandchild, Elizabeth, who was three years old at the time, a sing-along book titled "Away in a Manger." In our growing up years, "Away in a Manger" was and still is our most treasured song.

We wanted to give Elizabeth the book on Christmas Day, but we had to leave to return home that day. We did not want to miss seeing her reaction when she opened the present, so we decided to give it to her two days before Christmas.

We were surprised and absolutely amazed at how quickly she memorized the words to the song. Elizabeth sang the whole song with the sing-along book pressed tightly to her ear, making sure she was repeating the words recited to her. On Christmas morning, she had it down to a T.

Before leaving on Christmas day, we recorded Elizabeth on video, capturing every remarkable moment of her precious gestures while singing "Away in a Manger" with the sing-along book. Elizabeth sang as if she were singing unto the Lord in His presence.

This will always be a blessed memory of Elizabeth singing praises to our Lord Jesus Christ.

Luke 2:11-14 (CJB): "… This very day, in the town of David, there was born for you a Deliverer who is the Messiah, the Lord. Here is how you will know: you will find a baby wrapped in cloth and lying in a feeding trough." Suddenly, along with the angel was a vast army from heaven praising God: "In the highest heaven, glory to God! And on earth, peace among people of good will!"

23

Mercy protected us

In January 2013, my husband and I were viewing an infomercial opportunity we thought we might be interested in doing. This captured our interest because we were looking for ways to venture out with new ideas and increase our income. As we listened attentively, we tried to make sure we understood everything in its entirety. We thought we would jump on it and make an order.

After reviewing the infomercial several times, we felt this venture might possibly change some things for the better financially. In the infomercial they gave the name of the product and the price. The way it was explained on the infomercial is that you would be receiving several things that were included in the package.

We called the number that constantly flashed on the screen to make an order to receive the package. When we called, we thought it was suspicious that they immediately asked us for our credit card number without explaining what they would be sending.

We were starting to feel uncomfortable at this point but we continued on with the process. After giving the representative our credit card number, she explained what we had ordered, which was different from what the infomercial presented. The product they were offering on the telephone did not even come close to what they were offering on the infomercial.

We were becoming more nervous about the whole situation because we had given her our credit card number. The representative said that what we saw on the infomercial was an addition to the package we were ordering.

From that point on, nothing seemed to have clarity. She started going up on the prices of all the different packages, and nothing seemed to make sense because she was a fast talker, very aggressive, and rude.

So my husband and I decided that it was necessary to cancel the order. The representative said she could not cancel the order because the product had already gone out. We found this nonsense to be sinuous and crooked, but she was adamant about not refunding our money for a purchase we had done just minutes ago. She was so rude and unyielding and had the nerve to hang up on us.

We decided to call their customer service number to cancel. It was hard to believe that we could not cancel on the phone with her when we had just ordered. At this point, we were very concerned because this lady had our account information.

When we called customer service, we were told we had to wait 24 to 48 hours before they can pull up our account information. This was the last straw. Our thoughts were racing, not knowing what they were going to do with our information for 24 to 48 hours. My husband tried to explain what happened several times, telling them that what we saw on the infomercial did not comply with what the representative was saying on the phone.

We spoke with several customer representatives telling them how the representative who had taken the order was very rude and aggressive, and ignored my husband's questions. She kept on talking over him trying to upsell different products she stated would help us. The customer service representative listened, but there was nothing she could do because they could not pull up our account until it came through their system.

My husband and I waited 24 hours, and they still could not pull up anything. We were actually happy about this, but we wanted to keep checking. We waited for 48 hours, and they still could not pull up anything. We were really smiling hoping it did not go through.

We checked our account to see if any money had been taken. Nothing taken from our account. We called the infomercial customer service line every day and checked our account. Everything looked good.

One day when I called to see if the order had gone through, they had the audacity to ask me what my credit card number was in order to pull up my account. I emphatically said no. I could not believe they would ask me a question like that. Nothing has been taken out of our account, and we give glory and honor to our Lord Jesus Christ for protecting us.

Psalm 136:24 (ONM): And has redeemed us from our enemies, for His loving kindness endures forever.

24

Jesus' Peace saved the day

In January 2013, my husband and I were traveling to different stores to perform demonstrations showcasing a high tech blender for customers to buy on the spot.

We arrived and settled into our hotel to prepare for the next day. We rose up early the next day and went to the store, made veggie drinks and smoothies, demonstrating the features of the blender. Everything was going well. We made sales and completed our first day.

A couple of days went by, and suddenly, my husband was not feeling well. We decided to go to the emergency room to see what was going on. They recommended keeping him overnight. I was concerned about him. At the same time, we were scheduled to be at the store for a couple more days. We needed to quickly come up with a plan of action and resolve the problem.

Our company lined up these schedules out of town to feature their blender and demonstrate what it does. This happened to be our only source of income. My husband was the key person who demonstrated the blender, and I was his assistant. I had done some demonstrations, but I had always had my husband by my side. Performing in front of a crowd was not my cup of tea, but I managed to do it to support my husband.

We agreed that we had no other choice but for me to do the demonstrations until he was released from the hospital. Again, I normally assisted him with our shows, but I was never alone.

My nerves began to play a tune of fear, but I had to get hold of myself and knew what I had to do. I prayed to the Lord Jesus to help me, something I always tell my grandbaby Pearl to do when she is sad or in trouble. Sometimes it is easier said than done, but I knew I had to trust Jesus as I would want my grandbaby to trust Him.

Although no one was watching but the Lord, I had to be a witness in putting my total trust in Him. I asked Jesus to help me because my husband was in the hospital, and I was concerned about him.

The real kicker was that I had to drive in a city that was unfamiliar to me, and to top it off, I had to do these demonstrations without my husband being there. These things seemed so overwhelming and uncomfortable.

After presenting my concerns to the Lord, something so loving happened to me. Right at that moment, the Holy Spirit said to me, "Keep your mind on Me, and I will keep you in perfect peace."

I started praising the Lord Jesus, and His peace immediately quieted my spirit. I was able to focus on His Word and His goodness alone. An unexplainable calmness of God's love took over my being, exuding His confident presence and assuring me that He was there with me.

I did not care if I had to think on the same things over and over—His goodness, His grace, and how He rescued me in so many situations. Keeping my mind on Jesus truly kept me in perfect peace. To have experienced this truth in the middle of a stormy situation was a wonderful testimony for me. I know for sure that when you trust Jesus, He will never leave you nor forsake you.

For the two days that I was by myself, my husband would ask me if I was alright, and I would tell him yes, Jesus was with me the whole time. What was exciting was that I knew Jesus was with my husband as well, and I did not have to think about his situation of being in the hospital. Jesus assured me that my husband would be well taken care of and to keep my mind on Him.

When my husband got out of the hospital, he did not know, but all I could do was cry with thanksgiving. Jesus stuck close to me in my time of need, and I was so grateful and always will be. I kept saying, "Lord, You are so wonderful. You are my Rescuer!"

_____

Psalm 71:3 (ESV): Be to me a rock of refuge, to which I may continually come; you have given the command to save me, for you are my rock and my fortress.

25

Salvation at Sunset River Hotel

Once again, we were on an assignment traveling to another city to showcase the featured blender. After doing many shows, I needed a day off to relieve some of the stress one encounters after being on the feet thirteen hours a day.

We had a couple more days before our assignment ended. While I was taking it easy in the hotel room, the heater shut off. I did not know why it suddenly stopped working. I tried to adjust it, but nothing seemed to work, and the room was getting extremely cold, almost freezing.

Without hesitation, I trotted to the rental office to tell them about the heater. The manager's response was that we had to move to another room. My husband was at work, and I was thinking of the difficulty I would have trying to move all of our things to another room by myself. However, the cleaning crew graciously helped me.

After moving our things, I noticed a book I had been reading every day was missing. I knew exactly where I had placed it. I went to the other room we moved out of because the door was still open. Finding nothing there, I went back to the new room to look again. I found nothing.

At first, I was upset because I knew my book had been in the drawer, and my flesh wanted to make a big deal out of it. I was thinking about calling the office, but the Holy Spirit stopped me and said, "Do not call the office. Ask the lady who helped you move the things out of the drawer. Ask if she had seen the book."

I went down the stairs to the laundry room and politely described what the book looked like and asked if she had seen it. She responded that she had not seen it but insisted she would help me look for it. We went back upstairs and looked in the room we moved out of and again looked in the new room, but we found nothing.

Then, out of the blue, the Holy Spirit instructed me to ask her if she was saved. I'm thinking to myself: *Right now we're looking for the book, and You want me to ask her if she is saved?*

I obeyed the Holy Spirit and did what I was instructed to do. I gazed right into her eyes and asked, "Are you saved?" She replied no. I asked if she wanted to receive Jesus as her Lord and Savior because He will be coming soon.

She started talking about her grandmother being saved, so I interrupted her and once again asked the initial question: *Would you like to give your life to Jesus.*

I told her my testimony of how Jesus had provided for my husband and me when our house foreclosed, and we had no money to move and no place to go. I explained how Jesus provided resources that we could never have thought of, and that His ways are higher than our ways, and His thoughts are higher than our thoughts.

She said she was homeless and wanted to receive Jesus as her Savior and she believed He died on the Cross for her and she believed that He is the Son of God. She repented of her sins and received the Holy Spirit.

I laid hands on her and declared healing that had already been given to her through the blood of Jesus. I declared that Jesus had already gone ahead of her and made provisions for her and her family for a place to live. I advised her to find a church that believes Jesus is the Son of God and that teaches the truth. I assured her that this will help her know how to live for Jesus.

We embraced one another as she parted with tears of joy believing Jesus had already provided for her and her family. As she walked away, I was amazed at how God planned all of this using the heater not working and a lost book. My spirit was pouring out with worship and thanksgiving. God's plan was accomplished on that day, and I will always be grateful He used me to fulfill it.

Mark 1:15 (ESV): … and saying, "The time is fulfilled, and the kingdom of God is at hand; repent and believe in the gospel."

26

Bought laptop case, then received laptop by faith

In 2008, I went to a consignment store in Fayetteville, Georgia, just to browse around. I suddenly spotted a beautiful leather laptop case. I knew its value would have been at least $200.00 or more in a store. Whoever had the laptop case prior to putting it up to be sold had kept it in mint condition.

I was contemplating buying it, but guess what? I did not have a laptop, nor did I come close to being able to afford one. I continued to browse around while keeping the laptop case in my hand. I kept thinking to myself, *I don't know when I'll be getting a laptop, but I would love to have one.*

The lady who worked at the shop said someone had just recently dropped it off. Gee! What she said did not make my decision easier, but then, in a way, it did help me to make up my mind. I knew if I did not buy the laptop case that day, it would be gone in a snap.

To clinch my decision, I started looking at all of the different compartments inside this heavy duty, one-hundred-percent leather laptop case. Then I took it further, imagining how I would feel toting it to business meetings. My thoughts were wowing me and getting me excited about purchasing my find.

Okay, enough was enough. I decided to buy the leather laptop case because I knew that someday I would have a laptop. Before I came across this great deal, I had expressed many times that I would like to have a laptop someday. So I bought it, took it home, and put it in a safe place to maintain its good condition. There were times when my husband wanted to use it for business, but I said an emphatic NO, that is for my laptop!

Although I did not know when I would be getting a laptop, I knew in my heart that I would have one in the near future.

Several years ago, my mother had a laptop that was passed down to her from my aunt who lives in Florida. She was thrilled when she received it, and it seemed like she was on it every day and night. I was still without a laptop, but I knew strongly that I would have a laptop one day.

In November of 2012, my grandmother told me something and asked me to keep it confidential from my mother. I could not believe what my ears were hearing. My grandmother had bought my mother a new laptop.

Suddenly, my eyes widened, and my jaw dropped. I had something in mind. Yes! I'm going to ask my mother for her laptop after my grandmother gives her the new one. I closed my eyes tight, raised my hands, and said a big thank you to Jesus! I was walking by faith because I did not know if my mother would have plans for her old laptop, but I knew this was my opportunity to see if it was possible.

The time came when my grandmother told my mother about the laptop she had bought her for Christmas. I asked my mother if I could have her old laptop, and her answer was yes. My husband transferred her files to her new laptop, and the old one was mine!

Some may ask, "You were that excited over an old laptop?" Yes, I was excited and grateful to see Jesus' faithfulness and love in giving me what my heart desired. I believe Jesus knew this laptop would be used for His glory typing this book that He put in my heart.

Matthew 25:21 (ESV): "His master said to him, 'Well done, good and faithful servant. You have been faithful over a little; I will set you over much. Enter into the joy of your master.'"

27

A memorable character of Jesus revealed through a smile

My husband and I were doing blender demonstrations at a well-known local store in Murfreesboro, Tennessee. All of the demonstrators had to demonstrate their products for eleven days. One of the demonstrators representing another company came over to introduce herself. She was wearing a big smile.

There was something extremely peculiar about this lady. She was always gleaming and always smiling. Normally, when you are demonstrating a product, you keep a smile on your face, even if you do not want to. But, with this lady, there was a message luminously speaking and resonating her character in a beautiful way.

The first thought that came to my mind was that it was the Lord Jesus shining through her because I certainly experienced His presence whenever she would come over to our booth. Her demeanor was full of unrestrained enthusiasm and joy. Her peppiness and kindness magnetically stood out whether there was a crowd around her booth or not. And when you talked to her, you automatically transformed into this joyful smiling person.

When I got to know her, I found out that she was a believer in Jesus Christ and was saved. This did not surprise me at all. It was evident in her character. She said she was very active in the church and enjoyed serving the Lord.

She and I started taking our breaks at the same time to fellowship. We took turns praying every day over our lunch, and that jump-started our conversations talking about Jesus and His goodness. We shared testimonies about His faithfulness in our lives. She talked about how she loves to make banana bread for the church every Sunday morning.

What she said next sealed the deal for me of her love for Christ in how she exemplifies Him. She stated that every morning before she goes to the store to do her demonstrations, she prays for every employee at the local store and all of the demonstrators to be protected, to be blessed, and God would provide for all their needs. When she told me this, all I could think of was the selfless compassion she had toward others, which so resembled Jesus when He laid down His life for us. He did not think about Himself at all.

How wonderful to see Jesus exemplified through one of His children. When thoughts of Jesus are triggered through someone else's character, it is truly amazing. What a breath of fresh air to experience Jesus' love through another of His children. Her character of Christlikeness will always be remembered in my mind and in my spirit.

Thank you, Jesus, for your witnesses upon the earth. Hallelujah!

---

1 John 3:23-24 (ESV): And this is His commandment that we believe in the name of His Son Jesus Christ and love one another, just as He has commanded us. Whoever keeps his commandments abides in God, and God in him. And by this we know that he abides in us, by the Spirit whom he has given us.

28

Jesus' love expressed in a local store

Blessings of love sometimes come in peculiar and unfamiliar ways. My husband and I were, as usual, tending to our booth and doing demonstrations with the featured blender.

As my husband continued to do the demonstrations, I was talking to some of the customers out in the audience. I came across a lady named Ellen who stopped me and started talking about how she came to know Jesus. I did not know why Ellen decided to share her testimony when the reason for being there was to see the demonstration and buy blenders.

As Ellen shared her testimony with intensity, I began to be drawn in to the excitement she had of knowing Jesus. She was so enthusiastic that people were able to see her hand and arm gestures.

Ellen dove right in to her testimony claiming she was a cussing, fussing, hell raiser at one time. She declared that she would pick a fight with a man my husband's size or bigger and body slam him. Ellen stated that she used to be 300 pounds and was not afraid of anybody. She would get sloppy drunk and cuss everybody out.

As Ellen was disclosing all of these deplorable involvements, I thought to myself that nobody could possibly be this way. But she was serious and withholding nothing. I believe Ellen wanted to make known to me Jesus' mercy and grace that made her free. When she was explaining all of this, she was very close to my face, looking me right in my eyes.

After Ellen told me those things, she paused, stared into my eyes, and said that when she went to church, she felt uncomfortable and ashamed because she did not have the proper clothes to wear. She thought the people looked down on her, and they did until the preacher gave a sermon on the love of Jesus. He said that no matter the condition, Jesus does not show favoritism.

By this time, Ellen and I were hugging each other with joy. Then Ellen's most wonderful ending words were, "Jesus totally saved me."

As Ellen finished her testimony, she said she left church a different person that day, and on her way home, she called her husband and told him she would not be drinking anymore and not to bring any beer home. She told all of her friends she would not be going to the clubs anymore and that she would now be living for Jesus. Ellen said she was made new and totally different from the person she had been before. The next time she attended church, all the people who had looked down on her bought her lots of new clothes.

Then, as if a hummingbird was singing a sweet song in that local store, Ellen started singing the sweetest song of Jesus' love. With gratitude, she was singing the song to me about Jesus. By that time, neither of us thought about where we were or who was watching. It was Jesus and us. Ellen sang the whole song with gratitude and adoration.

She sang two more songs about how Jesus changed her. By that time, my eyes watered because I felt her freedom from all the bondage that satan used to keep her bound. She said satan is a liar and sang another song about how Jesus is everywhere she goes. Her sincere love for Jesus was expressed so deeply in her songs, and the words penetrated into the love of Jesus in my heart.

Ellen mentioned that her friends do not want to be around her anymore, but she's not discouraged because Jesus saved her, and He will save them, too. Ellen's last words were that she is born again and waiting for Jesus' coming, and she is going to continue to sing of His love until He comes. Hallelujah!

About an hour later, a sweet lady in her senior years who was driving a handicap cart stopped at our booth. She slowly got out of the cart and leaned over my table to tell me something. I leaned over, and being up close and looking me in my eyes, she also starting singing a loving song about Jesus. I broke down and cried because I felt overwhelming love from both of these ladies who expressed love for Jesus and me.

Later, I pondered how I saw Jesus visibility through all three women in that local store. These women expressed the importance of knowing Jesus and sharing with everyone you come in contact with about Jesus' love. This was the last day of our assignment and the most beautiful day in Murfreesboro, Tennessee.

What a wonderful going-away blessing sharing Jesus' love from His beloved children. Hallelujah!

Luke 15:24 (ESV): "For this my son was dead, and is alive again; he was lost, and is found." And they began to celebrate.

29

Forever grateful for Jesus' protection

My husband and I traveled to Macon, Georgia, to demonstrate a blender at a local major store. When we arrived in Macon, we stopped to get our hotel room where we would stay for the duration of our schedule.

We unloaded all of our things at the hotel, and then we went to set up our booth for the next day. When we finished, it was about two or three o'clock in the morning. We went back to the hotel to get some sleep because we had to get up early in the morning and go back to the store to do our demonstrations.

When we woke up the next morning, I was exhausted and could not keep my eyes open, so I asked my husband if I could stay at the hotel and go to work the next day. He responded yes and went off to work as I went back to bed.

About two hours later, I heard an alarmingly hard knock on my door. It startled me awake. I peeped through the peephole, and it was the manager saying, "Safety check." I responded, "Excuse me?" and he repeated, "Safety check." Well, I did not know if I heard him correctly, but it was hard to believe he was doing a safety check so early in the morning.

I remembered his face from the day before when we checked in, so I immediately put on my street clothes. When I was fully dressed, I opened the door, and he said he was doing a safety check. I found that quite odd, but I let him in.

He walked in the door and did something so inappropriate that I was frozen with fear. He closed the door quickly and locked both locks on the door. I backed up in fear asking myself what this man was doing. He did not see me back up, but he checked the microwave, opened all the cabinet doors, checked the lights in the rest room and refrigerator, then immediately unlocked both locks to the door and walked out.

While he was there, my heart was beating so fast because I felt like I had made a big mistake, and I feared I would not be able to get out of it. I had allowed a strange man to enter my room because he said he needed to do a safety check.

When he walked out that door, I locked both locks immediately. I took a deep breath, shaking like a leaf, but was relieved it was over.

I called my husband and told him what had happened. My husband was furious and said he was going to confront the manager. I convinced him not to, as we had to stay there a few more days. I was so nervous I asked my husband to pick me up. He left the store immediately to pick me up, but on his way, he stopped by the police department and told the police what had happened. The police said that room should have been inspected before it was leased out to anyone, and it seemed suspicious.

My husband was suspicious because the manager told him before we checked in that he had inspected the place already.

I believe sometimes when someone may be out to do you harm, God intervenes and encamps His angels round about us. In my spirit, I believe that is what happened to me. Jesus made His love visible to me and rescued me that day, and I will be forever grateful for His protection.

---

2 Thessalonians 3:2-3 (NLT): Pray, too, that we will be rescued from wicked and evil people, for not everyone is a believer. But the Lord is faithful; he will strengthen you and guard you from the evil one.

30

Never assume they won't be ready to share Christ

My husband and I were scheduled to travel to Macon, Georgia, to demonstrate a featured blender. As he was demonstrating the features on the blender, I was doing what I normally do, which is communicating with the customers to get feedback regarding this blender.

As I was talking with some of the people, one lady named Tina made it known she was very interested in the blender, so I directed my attention to discussing the benefits of owning this blender. Although Tina was interested in the blender, she made it known in the conversation that she did not have the money at the time.

As Tina and I got past the blender conversation, she began relating to me that she had just got saved and was extremely happy. But she also was encountering issues with her boyfriend. She conveyed to her boyfriend that she got saved, and he responded he was happy for her. But Tina began to notice a change in his behavior toward her. He started speaking harshly and belittling her, discouraging the hopes and dreams she was planning.

Tina made it clear to me that she still loved him, but he had moved on. At this point, I thought I would take a shot at asking Tina a pivotal question. I inquired if she had asked her boyfriend if he would like to receive Jesus Christ as his Lord and Savior because Jesus loves him, too.

Then Tina made a statement my ears could not believe, especially after she had expressed the joy she felt after being born again. "He's not ready," she announced."

I purposely stared at her with a question as seriously equal as her unfair judgment. "How can you assume he's not ready?" Her answer was, of course, painted by how he was mistreating her at the time.

I explained to Tina that Jesus is always waiting for us to turn to Him. I posed a question to her so that she could think about how she would feel if someone thought she was not ready. She would have missed the most wonderful opportunity for salvation. I reiterated by asking, "What if someone looked at us and said we're not ready and did not share Jesus Christ with us?" I explained to her that whether a person says yes or no, everyone is in need of a Savior who loves them.

With water in her eyes, she said she understood. I also explained that the reason she and her boyfriend were having problems now was because light and darkness cannot fellowship. What Tina did not realize is that not only did he move on, but she did as well when she accepted Jesus Christ as her Lord. I expressed to Tina to always be ready to share the love of Jesus Christ with those who are lost. We are to always stay in awareness of lost people around us. To share Christ with the lost is wanting them to experience His love and to live in His presence forever.

Let us keep in the forefront of our minds that we are to proclaim the Good News of Jesus Christ and His resurrection to others, breaking every bondage through repentance. The driving force of all believers should be wanting to see the salvation of the Lord Jesus and His glorious works in saving the lost. Hallelujah!

Isaiah 61:1 (ESV): The Spirit of the Lord GOD is upon me, because the LORD has anointed me to bring good news to the poor; he has sent me to bind up the brokenhearted, to proclaim liberty to the captives, and the opening of the prison to those who are bound; ...

31
Thankfulness got Jesus' attention

My husband woke up one morning and realized he needed to renew his driver's license by the next day, which was his birthday. How this had slipped his mind I do not know.

This last minute transaction brought about finding out via the internet that there were new laws put in place regarding documentation to get his license. He decided to call DDS in Georgia, and one of the documents he needed was his birth certificate.

We did not know where the birth certificate was or if we would be able to find it in time, since his birthday was the next day. We searched everywhere we could think of looking, but we were unsuccessful in finding it.

We started backtracking its whereabouts when we moved from one place to another. We were thinking it might be in storage but hoping it was not because we did not want to dig through all of those boxes. What made things more challenging and pressured was that my husband had to drive to Macon, Georgia, to work the next day.

So my husband decided we would get up early the next morning and go and explain our dilemma to the DDS license office. We felt like there was nothing else we could do, so we stopped searching.

While I was in the kitchen cleaning a cooking pot, I was thanking the Lord for my salvation, for providing for us, and I went on and on with gratitude. By this time, I was not thinking about the birth certificate.

Suddenly, the Holy Spirit said, "Look in the spot where you keep your important papers." I have a spot where I keep all of my important papers, memorable things my son did when he was small, memorable greeting cards from my mom, and the list goes on.

I went straight to the spot, looked and looked, and then finally found his birth certificate. I lifted up my hands with water in my eyes and said, "Thank you, Father, Son, and Holy Spirit for being here when we need You."

That day, I witnessed something valuable: being thankful definitely got Jesus' attention and will bring you exactly what you need. Thanking Jesus keeps you in awareness and remembrance of His goodness toward you and toward others upon the earth.

Thank you, Jesus, for supplying what we needed. Hallelujah!

Psalm 50:23 (ESV): The one who offers thanksgiving as his sacrifice glorifies me; to one who orders his way rightly I will show the salvation of God!"

32

Listen, the Holy Spirit is talking

One evening, Charlotte, my husband, and I went out to dinner celebrating my husband's birthday. We were having a grand time because we had not seen Charlotte in quite a while. She worked long hours in her profession, and so did my husband and I.

As we were enjoying our dinner and fellowship, I discerned a heavy, hurt, and burdened spirit in Charlotte. At the time, I did not know why she was experiencing this uneasiness.

All of a sudden, something came over me, and I knew what it meant to be a part of the Body of Christ while experiencing those same feelings. At that moment, I felt everything she was feeling, the heaviness, the hurt, and the burdened spirit. I believe the reason I was allowed to feel Charlotte's distress was so I would know how to encourage her in the Lord Jesus Christ.

After we finished our dinner, we embraced and went to our separate cars. When my husband and I arrived home, I got in the shower, and immediately the Holy Spirit said I was to tell Charlotte that she is a leader and not a follower, except that she is to follow Christ Jesus. He said as long as she continues to be a follower of men, she will have problems. The Lord told me to tell Charlotte she is a leader and has been called to lead. There are people who will follow Christ through her leadership.

When I related this to Charlotte at 12:20 AM, she said she was feeling so downcast. Charlotte said she knew I had to have heard from the Lord because on her way home after leaving the restaurant, she was in deep conversation asking the Lord what she should do. She did not know what to do about her situation. She said she was asking the Lord what He wanted her to do for Him because she wanted to please Him.

Charlotte thanked me for my obedience. My reply was that I would not have been able to sleep until I told her what the Holy Spirit had said.

My experience at that moment reminded me of how Christ Jesus feels when we are troubled by situations. Jesus encourages and reminds us of His Word giving us peace that goes beyond our understanding.

Hallelujah!

---

2 Corinthians 1:4 (NLT): He comforts us in all our troubles so that we can comfort others. When they are troubled, we will be able to give them the same comfort God has given us.

33

No strangers in the body of Christ

It is so wonderful seeing Jesus in His people everywhere you go. Elliott and I were working at a common store in Macon, Georgia, for two weeks when we met a beautiful couple named Ben and Laura who had stopped to see our demonstration.

After the demonstration was over, we introduced ourselves. From there we knew God had put us together as believers. Ben and Laura's zeal was evident with a drawing love for Christ Jesus and others. They boasted about the Word of God and its everlasting truth with exuberance and adoration.

We all expressed our deepest compassion to reach those who are lost and to wake up the sleeping believers out of their comfort zones to be revived for Christ Jesus. We expressed our desire to proclaim the Good News, heal the sick, raise the dead, and encourage God's children to come together to live a life of seeing the Salvation of the Lord upon the earth.

As we were attesting to God's goodness and mercy through His Son Jesus Christ, it was obvious that we were all in one accord regarding God's Word. What great joy it is to meet sisters and brothers in Christ going in the same direction as Christ.

My husband and I knew this because it is our goal and that of many others. Followers of Christ are noticeable among believers who are going in the same direction. Let us keep following Christ Jesus, and we will gladly see others along the way.

We exchanged information with our new friends and agreed to stay in touch and fellowship with one another. Just before leaving, Ben and Laura prayed a prayer of love over our business, our lives, and for a safe trip back home. What a beautiful witness they were of Christ and His Light shining through them.

We embraced with holy kisses like we had known each other all our lives. I am convinced there are no strangers in the Body of Christ. It is everlasting love that comes straight from the throne of God. Thank You, Jesus, for my sisters and brothers in Christ Jesus. Hallelujah!

Ephesians 2:19 (ESV): So then you are no longer strangers and aliens, but you are fellow citizens with the saints and members of the household of God ...

34

Love won, rebellion lost

When I was fifteen years old, I was hired as a recreational leader at a recreational park in Cocoa, Florida. During the summers, jobs were provided for teens, but in order to work at that age, we had to have a work permit signed by the county and our parents.

I was inspired about working there because it gave me the opportunity to buy my clothes for the school year. As a recreational leader, my duties were to organize summer activities for the children ages seven and eight. Something memorable happened there that will always remind me Jesus was there directing my steps at that young age.

While organizing the activities for the children, there was one little girl named Zoe who was about seven years old. She was a bully, and I mean a threatening bully. Even as a young teenager, I was intimidated by Zoe's threats. Zoe would say what she was going to do to me and the kids at the end of the day.

Those threats went on for weeks. In my young age, I did not have a clue what to do. I must admit there were times I was afraid, but something inside me did not want to give up on the children. I was drawn close to the children, and, through their actions, they were drawn close to me.

I really started observing Zoe's behavior and noticed that she seemed very unhappy and very angry. She was rebellious and did not want anyone to tell her what to do. She started causing disruptions among the group during the class. I knew something had to be done because Zoe was terrorizing the other children.

Before we would play softball, I would have the children form a straight line. Then Zoe would cut in front of the children, pushing them to get behind her. Also, if we were playing dodge ball, Zoe would grab the ball and hold on to it.

I found out something interesting about Zoe. She did not live far from the recreation center. I started investigating and was told she would wander off from home whenever she wanted, and at times, no one knew where she was.

Then what really shocked me was that Zoe was never signed up for the recreation program. She would just show up there as if she was a part of the program. Once the information became evident that she was not enrolled in the program, I had to find out why she was there every day.

Although Zoe was mean and rebellious, I did not have the heart to have someone escort her off the property just because she was not on the roster for the summer program. So I decided to bear with her for a little while until I found a resolution for the problem. Then I began to look at the whole situation from a different perspective.

Zoe was crying for help, attention, and love. I did not know the Holy Spirit was guiding and using me at that time. All I knew was love took over my mind and heart for Zoe.

A couple of weeks before summer camp ended, I decided to allow Zoe to take part in leadership with the children. Zoe's responsibility was to make sure everything went smoothly with all the activities. I gave her the responsibilities of making sure the children lined up in a straight line. She had to designate someone to get the balls and bats for softball, put up the softballs when finished, get them prepared for swimming, and the list went on.

When we were approaching the end of summer camp, I noticed Zoe's demeanor had utterly changed. She was not bullying anyone, she was not disrupting the class, and the tone of her voice was pleasant. Zoe was asking me if she could do anything else for me. Suddenly, Zoe was kind, helpful, and loving.

This change in Zoe was a resemblance of Christ Jesus living and shining in me. And what was most loving about Zoe at the end of the summer camp was that she did not want to leave my side. She stayed right by me until I left the recreational center.

But before leaving, I told her I was very proud of her, and she was very special to me. I encouraged Zoe and told her she was smart and could be whatever she want to be in life. I thanked her for helping me with summer camp and gave her a big hug.

She asked if I would be there next summer, and I told her I did not know. She responded that she hoped I would be there next year. I gave her another hug, and then we parted.

In my youth, I knew something great had happened both to Zoe and to me that we would always reflect and smile about. Thank you, Christ Jesus, for using me at a young age to show love to a little girl who desperately needed to know she was loved. Love won her over and made her a caring person. Thank You, Jesus, for using me for Your Glory!

John 13:35 (ESV): "... By this all people will know that you are my disciples, if you have love for one another."

35

A thankful heart transformed their heart

I remember seeing Jesus so visibly and in His love making His presence known to me. One particular year, someone very close to me named Anita was visiting. When Anita visited, which was not too often, it was always a pleasure seeing her. She was not staying with us but was staying at Melissa and Trina's house.

Anita had been here several days before my husband and I had a chance to visit with her. We ended up going a couple of times to enjoy visiting with them all. But there was one particular day when something special happened that will always be remembered.

My husband had things he had to tend to this particular day, so I asked him to drop me off to socialize with the ladies. We usually had a blast when we all got together, giving each another updates about ourselves.

I called, giving them heads up that I would be dropping by, and of course, they were excited. Or, at least, they seemed to be excited.

I knocked on the door, and when I walked in, it was completely silent, as if something had been said, and they did not want me to know about it. I walked in slowly and carefully embraced everyone. Although I was experiencing uncertain feelings, I proceeded to join in as though nothing was wrong.

My spirit was speaking loud and clear that they were talking about something that was not to be revealed because, usually, when I arrived, the responses were loving and joyful.

Their displeasing dispositions were so strong that if my husband had not driven off so fast, I would have stopped him, politely excused myself, and had him drive me back home. However, I had to move forward greeting everyone kindly and cautiously because I did not know where I stood with them at the moment.

After acknowledging each one, I said a few words and excused myself to the guest room where my husband and I usually lodged when we stayed there. I closed the door and started offering my Father God, through His Son Jesus Christ, sacrifices of praise and thanksgiving. I worshipped Him, sang songs unto Him, and thanked Him for everything I could think of with gladness. Jesus' love assured me I had nothing to be concerned about because He was there.

Upon finishing my worship, I was refreshed and filled with Jesus love. Every disappointing and uncomfortable feeling had melted away as though it had gone out to the sea. I walked out with the biggest smile on my face and went to the kitchen because I was designated to season and cook the turkey for Thanksgiving.

While I was in the kitchen preparing the turkey, I continued singing praises unto the Lord Jesus Christ while everyone was in the living room. As I was singing unto the Lord and seasoning the turkey, something astonishing happened. Anita came to me and put money in my hand. I was completely stunned and speechless but was able to softly utter the words, "Thank you."

But it did not end there. Everyone else started getting up and asking me if they could help me with anything. It was as if God started everything from the beginning the way it was meant to be, with us loving one another.

I saw Jesus transform all of our hearts, and it was all done through worship and thankfulness that miraculously changed the setting of our fellowship and made it a beautiful evening of love.

Praises to our Father through His Son, Jesus Christ, Who transforms hearts and brings wonderful endings. Hallelujah!

Deuteronomy 10:21 (ONM): He is your praise and He is your God, Who has done these great and awesome things for you, which your eyes have seen.

36

Each one reach one

One of my favorite heartfelt songs was written and sung by a known singer from my former church. I heard him sing it when my son and I first moved to Marietta, Georgia, in 1990. The most beautiful act of love happened on the second day of our arrival.

Our neighbors, Lindsey and family, brought over a pie to greet and welcome us to the area. I was taken by surprise and touched by this gesture because where we had moved from in Northern Virginia, it seemed like a crime to even greet your neighbor. Living there felt as if you were invisible.

It was difficult to make friends, and I found it quite unsettling to continue to live there. People would say the reason they would not speak was because they were cautious. I thought it was a poor excuse for not being friendly neighbors or to say a simple hello. I was raised to greet your neighbors. It was respectful among those who lived around you or people you came in contact with.

Our new neighbor, Lindsey, invited us to church in Marietta, off of Roswell Road, the same church the known singer attended. At the time, I had never heard of the singer, but before I attended the church, Lindsey was telling me about her with excitement.

My son, John, and I started attending the church, and everyone was so kind. John and I adored Sunday school and church services. On Wednesdays before service, they served in the fellowship hall with everyone breaking bread together. The experience was unimaginable.

When my son and I attended services, I always enjoyed hearing the singer. But there was one song that was awe-inspiring to me right up to this day. The lyrics to this particular song titled "Each One Reach One" are the most beautiful I have ever heard. Back then, they were selling cassette tapes, and I must have played that song a million times. I would play it in my house, in my car, everywhere I went. It was like I could not get enough of it.

I believe the Holy Spirit was ministering to my heart at the time because I would sing along and be sobbing with tears. That song captivated my heart with the love of Christ Jesus until a sudden peace and a mountain of worship and thanksgiving would overtake me.

Even as I write about the wonderful experience of this song, it still has the same effect, putting me right into the presence of our Savior, Jesus Christ. This song explains clearly what the Body of Christ should be doing to please the Father through Jesus.

This song, "Each One Reach One," embodies the direction in which our lives should be led by proclaiming the Good News of Christ Jesus. Hallelujah!

Isaiah 52:7 (CJB): How beautiful on the mountains are the feet of him who brings good news, proclaiming *shalom*, bringing good news of good things, announcing salvation and saying to Tziyon, "Your God is King!"

37

Jesus did not blame my shame

I was sitting in my living room mediating on the Lord when the Holy Spirit told me to write down my testimony. The Holy Spirit said to tell the people what you used to be ashamed of and that I had delivered you. I paused and thought about it for a moment. Then I realized that this was part of my being released from the silence of my shame.

Sometimes we can be delivered but still silently struggle, which means we are still entangled with the shame. Sharing our testimony with others of how God delivered us of our shame makes us free. As well, those listening to our testimony can be made free.

Our testimony causes the listeners to feel free and safe to come to Christ, to put all of their trust in Him, and to follow Him for the rest of their lives. They will come to the Lord Jesus with repentance because they heard what He did for us, and they want the same release.

You see, I allowed this masturbation spirit to ensnare me. I was captured by it once upon a time. This defiling spirit had me trapped in its shameful lust, and I did not know how to get out of it. I always felt dirty and defiled after the shameful act because I knew God saw me. I knew I could not hide my lustful act from Him. It was like being trapped in an addictive act of darkness with no light at the end of the tunnel.

One day, I became tired of being trapped in this jail of masturbation that was taking me down to its ruins. I cried out to the Lord and said, "Jesus, help me. I want this out of my life, and I do not have the strength to do it myself." I cried out to the Lord like a baby, wanting to get out of this vicious, unbecoming cycle. My Lord and Savior, Jesus Christ, heard my cry. He knew the desire of my heart wanting desperately to get out of this prison of sin.

Immediately, Jesus reminded me of my freedom through His precious blood on the Cross, His resurrection, and how this entrapment was laid upon Him. Jesus did not blame my shame. He gave me peace.

Resting in Jesus Christ from this ensnared act of masturbation forever changed my life. Now, openly, without shame, this is my testimony of my freedom. Hallelujah!!

Psalm 3:4 (NLT): I cried out to the LORD, and he answered me from his holy mountain.

Hebrews 12:2 (CJB): ... looking away to the Initiator and Completer of that trusting, Yeshua – who, in exchange for obtaining the joy set before him, endured execution on a stake as a criminal, scorning the shame, and has sat down at the right hand of the throne of God.

38

Holy Spirit revealed plans

This day was glorious, and I was about to find out why. My husband and I decided to cook for my grandmother who would be 89 years old in June. I told my husband she loved spaghetti, so he said he would make home-cooked spaghetti and meatballs for her from scratch.

He and I collaborated to make this diner special and enjoyable. We decided to invite Melissa and Trina to join us, making our gathering a family feast. Before we left our house, Melissa called and suggested that we have Bible study. I responded okay.

My grandmother was in her senior years, and we realized it was a blessing to serve her with love. We all went over to Grandmother's house, and my husband started seasoning the meat with some good ole herbs and then added some vegetables. I did the easy part of boiling the angel hair spaghetti, and my mother watched over the garlic bread.

While they were finishing up the dinner, I went to the store and bought some vanilla ice cream, so we could put our bananas and chocolate chip cookies in it.

After the food had finished cooking, we all sat down and blessed the food. When we took our first bite, all of our faces were filled with expressions of "Mmmmm, ooooh this is so good."

Elliott, my husband, really put his heart into it, and believe me, the flavor of the spaghetti spoke for itself. My grandmother said, "Elliott, this is the best spaghetti I've ever had." *Are you kidding me,* I thought to myself. Can you imagine how much spaghetti she's had in her lifetime? What an inspiring compliment.

After finishing our delicious food, we teamed up and washed the dishes. We were preparing to start our Bible study when my grandmother asked me a surprising question. "Angela, how can I remember the Scriptures after I finish reading them in the Bible?" At that moment, the Holy Spirit took over and helped me to answer in a way she could understand.

I called my grandmother "Mama," so I said, "Mama, faith comes by hearing the Word of God." My grandmother has an electronic Bible, so she can read and listen to it at her leisure. I said, "Mama, when you keep hearing the Word of God, then whenever you need Him, His Word will be brought back to your remembrance. Before you start reading and listening to your electronic Bible, ask the Holy Spirit for wisdom, revelation, and understanding, and He will give it to you." She said okay.

Then the Holy Spirit directed me to do something I had not planned. I stood up and walked over to my grandmother, laid my hands on her, and asked the Holy Spirit to bring His Word to her remembrance that she would be given wisdom, revelation, and understanding in His Word.

Earlier that day, my grandmother had said she had pain in her eyes. So I rebuked the pain from her eyes and decreed her deliverance that was done through Christ Jesus' blood—His death, burial, and resurrection.

Boldness through the power of the Holy Spirit had taken over my body to do the plans of the Lord unashamedly. The Holy Spirit assured me I will be doing more of this for many to come.

My grandmother was praising the Lord, and I give Him all the glory and praise in using me for His plans.

We continued our Bible study, joyfully being in the presence of the Lord. We all gave each other Holy kisses and parted with love.

We took Melissa home, and she asked us to call her when we got home because it was late. I called Melissa when we arrived home, and she said something humbling I had never heard her say. She affirmed, "Angela, you are truly a woman of God."

Thank you, Jesus. I am in Your plans. Hallelujah!

Jeremiah 29:11 (CJB): "… 'For I know what plans I have in mind for you,' says *Adonai*, 'plans for well-being, not for bad things; so that you can have hope and a future …'"

39

Taste a little salt

We always look forward to celebrating Resurrection Day, the day we commemorate the resurrection of our Lord and Savior, Jesus Christ. Just thinking about it brings much joy and freedom for our lives.

This particular year, our relatives gathered for dinner after the church service, which was my grandmother's first Resurrection Sunday (Easter Sunday) living in Georgia. We had a great feast, laughing and enjoying each another.

After everything was over, we all stayed overnight with my grandmother, except for Trina. My grandmother was thrilled that we were staying. She loves company, especially family.

After everything was over, I set the alarm on my phone, and we all went to sleep. When my alarm went off the next morning, I felt pain across my belly area as I got up to turn it off. I wondered if it was something I ate or if I had eaten too much, I could not figure it out.

I went to the restroom to freshen up, and I heard the Holy Spirit say, "Go taste a little salt." I went to my grandmother's cabinet, put a little salt in the palm of my hand, took my finger, and tasted the salt. Instantly, my stomach felt better.

With excitement and raising up my hands, I thanked the Lord for His wonderful love and His instruction that healed me instantly. How wonderful it is to have the help of the Holy Spirit and to see God's miraculous works right before your eyes.

The more I listen and obey the Holy Spirit, the more I trust and see His presence in my everyday life. Hallelujah!

_____

Psalm 46:9 (CJB): Come and see the works of A*DONAI*, the astounding deeds he has done on the earth.

40

Favorable revelation illuminated my spirit

Some experiences lead us to life lessons we never forget. My husband and I had a disagreement, and I childishly stormed out of the room. I did not want to discuss what he wanted to talk about.

We did not talk to each other for a couple of hours. I knew my behavior was not right, but I allowed pride to stand up and take its place for a while. My flesh was enjoying the rudeness of walking out on my husband, but my spirit was smothering and drowning me with shame.

Later that night, while communicating with the Lord, I questioned Him what I should do. God is my Father, and I'm His daughter. I can ask Him anytime for direction because I know that when Father God gives me direction and I obey, He is pleased and glorified. And sometime, when I know I've done wrong, I have a loss of words as to what to say to make things right in His sight.

So I ask the Lord what I should do. The Holy Spirit said, "Go and get it right with him, then come back to Me." I said verbally out loud, "Yes, Sir." (I respond to the Holy Spirit this way when I'm being corrected.)

I got up and went to the bedroom. I told my husband that my behavior was inappropriate and asked if he would forgive me. My husband replied, "Yes." Then I went to the living room and asked Jesus to forgive me.

As I was repenting, the Holy Spirit declared, "You are to be a witness for Me to your husband, to always forgive him and ask to be forgiven."

When I heeded the Holy Spirit's instructions and asked for forgiveness from my husband and then asked Jesus to forgive me, His peace consumed me with gladness and joy. This favorable revelation illuminated my spirit and spoke loud and clear of God's goodness and love.

Whenever the Holy Spirit corrects and I obey, I am released from the bondage that stands in the way of God's goodness and mercy. This illuminated revelation, with obedience, puts us right back in His presence, pleasing Him as His little children. Hallelujah!

Romans 12:1 (ESV): I appeal to you therefore, brothers, by the mercies of God, to present your bodies as a living sacrifice, holy and acceptable to God, which is your spiritual worship.

41

Reminder of love in sadness

It was a beautiful day. The sun was out, and it was 65 degrees. I was determined to enjoy it. I told a lady named Maxine who works at the phone company that I would give her a pair of earrings free because she purchased some jewelry from me the day before.

I am a jewelry designer, which is a gift God gave me. I thank God for giving me the opportunity to serve in different capacities to honor and give Him glory in everything He would have my hands to do.

I made earrings for Maxine with her favorite colors she had made known to me and took them to her the next day. When I approached Maxine with the earrings, I told her she seemed to be very sad.

Maxine responded, "Yes, something is going on, but I'm fine now." She gazed at me with amazement saying it must have been a woman's intuition. I knew it was the Holy Spirit, but I was not led to reveal to her at that moment how I knew of her sadness.

In my spirit, I felt a need to make known to her that God loves her and always will. So I told her. I asked Maxine if she believed it. She responded yes and said that she needed to hear it. She needed to know God's love is everlasting and not like a light switch that can be turn on and off.

I informed Maxine that Jesus will be coming back very soon. He died on the Cross for her and now lives. Anytime she needs to talk to Jesus, He will be there for her. She smiled, gave me a big hug, and said thank you so much. We then parted ways.

Later on that day, the Holy Spirit spoke to me and confirmed, "Angela, it might not have seemed like the right timing because another person was at the counter, rap music was playing loud in the background, and it seemed like the atmosphere was not right, but when you say my name, Jesus, something happens, something changes. You may not be able to see it at that moment, and you may never know about it, but My Peace comes, and My Joy comes when My Name is proclaimed. Telling her I love her, and I always will, after what you picked up in your spirit, revealed to her that I AM still there for her always! Hallelujah!

---

1 John 3:23 (NASB): This is His commandment, that we believe in the name of His Son Jesus Christ, and love one another, just as He commanded us.

42

Do as I do

Someone called me and said a man who is very well known in gospel circles and is a public image on television is ill. I told the person I was not aware of it but I would look it up on the internet or ask my mother.

Twelve minutes later, the Holy Spirit said to me that when someone is ill, you do not have to go searching on the Internet or ask anyone to get more detail. You simply do what Jesus did.

Jesus said, "Come out! Loose that person!" The Holy Spirit continued speaking to me, "As My disciple, you are to do as I do, as I did on earth, and greater things. You are to tell the Good News, not spread tales about people's illnesses. Do not be conformed to this world's way of getting My work done!"

Hallelujah!

John 14:12 (CJB): Yes, indeed! I tell you that whoever trusts in Me will also do the works I do! Indeed, he will do greater ones, because I am going to the Father.

1 John 4:17 (CJB): Here is how love has been brought to maturity with us: as the Messiah is, so are we in the world. This gives us confidence for the Day of Judgment.

43

Discovered family

My sister, Jewel, who is a few years younger, told me that my stepmother, Leah, went to our grandparent's house and noticed a little girl sitting by herself. Leah inquired, "Who is this cute little girl?" She looked like Carson, Leah's husband. This was the beginning of something new for me and my discovered family.

Leah reached out in an attempt to get to know me, and I was getting to know my sisters. I can remember going over to my discovered family's house, and when I walked in, it was the most beautiful house I had ever seen. When I walked in the door, the living room was decorated beautifully, with pretty, decorative images on the walls. I remember sitting down near the dining room area.

I do not remember anyone telling me at that point that the two little girls were my sisters, but I'm sure we were told. I remember when I became aware that they were my sisters, I was the happiest girl in the world. Just to think I really had sisters, sisters I could play with, laugh with, and share things with. It all seemed so strange but exciting, and I can imagine it probably was a little awkward for them.

Then the fun began. Leah started picking me up on weekends to spend time with my sisters, Jewel and Harmony. I was anxious to get out of school on Fridays because I knew I would be picked up that evening, and

I looked forward to it.

Leah would pick me up to spend summers with my sisters as well. Leah was a lot of fun but very firm. When I became an adult I realized Leah had great balance in how she managed the household. Although she was firm, she kept fun activities going on for all of us sisters.

My sister, Jewel, and I still laugh about when we were young, how my stepmother Leah put Harmony, Jewel, and me in a majorette summer program. Being in this majorette program, they were preparing us to be in a parade. Jewel and I laughed so hard remembering being in the parade. I tripped first, and then my two sisters tripped because I tripped. Wow, that must have been the funniest thing to the audience and to Leah.

Also, I remember Leah putting us in tumbling classes, which made the summer enjoyable for us sisters. Leah was always active with us. As we got older, she would allow us to have dances with our friends at the house.

Jewel had a birthday party at their house. We had a smashing time, and there were plenty of people who attended, or at least it seemed that way. We were about 13 or 14 years old, and Jewel had a lot of friends from school and those who lived in the neighborhood at the party.

Another memorable thing was when my stepmother, Leah, would buy our summer clothes. She would buy these ruffled, pastel color panties and socks and lay them out on the bed. I know this may seem corny, but my sisters and I loved those beautiful pastel ruffled panties.

Another awesome experience I appreciated with Leah was what she would do with us sisters when we misbehaved. She would first sit us down, explain to us what we did, and why she was chastising us. Leah did this with so much love that we knew she loved us after the chastisement was over. This made us not want to do it again because of how it was lovingly done.

Sometimes I chuckle to myself because I remember Leah's voice when Jewel and I would try to go to the store without our little sister, Harmony. I did not mind, but Jewel would whisper to Harmony, "Go home." My stepmother would holler our names saying, "You better let her go with y'all."

I cannot possibly put into words all of the wonderful times I had with my discovered family, except to say thank you to this wonderful woman, Leah, who just simply inquired, "Who is this cute little girl?" Leah made my summers beautiful, joyful, and memorable.

Leah has always reminded me of the "Leave It To Beaver," kind of mother, nurturing, firm, smart, organized, loving, attentive, fun, and the list goes on.

Leah, thank you for the gift of love and experience you allowed me to see and reflect as an example of how I am to be now with my son and grandchildren. I will always love you and appreciate the experiences you shared with me.

Galatians 5:22-23 (NASB): But the fruit of the Spirit is love, joy, peace, patience, kindness, goodness, faithfulness, gentleness, self-control …

44

Grandmother gave glory to Jesus

Before my grandmother on my father's side passed, I was able to share the love of Christ Jesus with her on the telephone. She was excited to hear about Jesus and expressed her love for Him.

She thanked Jesus for the long life He had given her. She and I had a glorious time praising the Lord for all of His goodness.

Our praise and adoration for the Lord's goodness went on for a while. Then she paused and said, "I love you, Angela." She said she always felt so good when I called. She kept repeatedly saying she loved me.

I did not attend my grandmother's homegoing, but I will always remember her sweet words of adoration to the Lord for her life, and that in itself was the best homegoing for me to remember!

Hallelujah!

Philippians 1:21 (CJB): For to me, life is the Messiah, and death is gain.

45

Marsha's unstoppable faith

Marsha walked up to our table where a popular blender was being demonstrated. She watched it several times and was sold on all the features and impressed with how it pulverized vegetables, fruits, and grain.

Marsha called her husband and asked if she could buy the blender. He said no because of the price. Marsha was disappointed with her husband's decision, and it showed on her face.

But there was one thing about Marsha. She was so determined that she stuck around the demonstration table. She would wonder off to other parts of the store, but then she would pop up again asking questions, as if she wanted desperately to take a blender home.

Then Marsha started to ask if there was any other way she could buy the blender. We had one more day of demonstration, so we told her the next day would be the last day to purchase it.

Marsha made another call and still got hit with another deadend. She wondered off again for about 30 minutes, and then walked up to the counter to asked if she had any other options.

We spoke with the manager, and he said she could open up a store credit, but she said her husband would not agree to that. The store manager said that was the best he could do for her. Marsha's face turned bright red with discouragement and frustration, and you could see it in her eyes.

Marsha left the store feeling defeated about losing what she desired. I felt so helpless. I wanted to do something, but there was nothing I could do.

For some reason, out of all the people that came to our booth that day, there was something about Marsha's spirit that touched me, and I knew the Lord Jesus knew about it. Marsha stayed on my mind for the rest of the day and that evening.

When my husband and I retired from work that night and went to the hotel, he said, Angela, that lady really wanted that blender. Suddenly, with boldness and without hesitation, not even knowing I was going to say this, I said, "She's coming back to get that blender."

The Holy Spirit affirmed that it would come to pass, and I was super excited about it. Then God filled me with His peace, and I was able to rest.

The next day, which was Sunday, our last day of demonstration, I was standing in front of the booth speaking to someone to my left. My husband in a soft voice said, "Angela, look who is beside you."

I turned to my right, and there stood Marsha, the woman who desperately wanted that blender the day before. She was wearing the biggest and brightest smile I had seen. I reached out and gave her a big hug. She heard the excitement in my voice and saw my eyes as they became watery. I told her I was so glad to see her.

Marsha returned to get the blender she had longed for, and her face was shining and full of joy.

God reached out and gave the blender to her Himself.

Before Marsha left she started to explain why she needed a good blender. She was a former breast cancer patient. She had been wanting a blender that would juice carrots into liquid form, and when she saw our blender demonstration, she knew this was it.

After giving her testimony of Jesus healing her from breast cancer, I knew there was something more than her wanting to buy the blender. I was feeling something much more in my spirit.

Marsha proceeded to say that by drinking carrot juice, she was healed of breast cancer.

This time when she walked away, we all experienced the presence of the Lord and His faithfulness with unspeakable joy!

Hallelujah!

James 2:22 (ONM): You see that his faith was working together with his works and that faith was made complete by his works.

46

Offense, I send you away!

Someone close to me named Roy laughed when I told him I was a professional writer. He laughed hard. I knew he laughed because it was something foreign to his ears, and to a certain degree, it was to mine as well.

I knew it was important to start speaking the truth by faith, whether I was laughed at or encouraged. But what surprised me was that when Roy broke out in his hearty laugh, I was not offended. It was as if a shield of love and truth protected my heart. I became aware of what prepared me for this moment when I thought about what I had done prior to being laughed at.

Several weeks prior, I was listening to a pastor who was teaching on hindrances that will stop one from moving forward. Immediately, I knew for me, it was being easily offended. I admitted to myself that it was a deeply-rooted characteristic that stopped me from moving forward in many areas, such as relationships and works that I am called to do.

Through this pastor, there were instructions given. He said to write down everything that hinders you. Being easily offended by others was the first and most difficult one that I wanted desperately out of my life.

Then, the next phase we were to do was to demand what hinders us to get out of us. Every time it tried to creep up, I thanked God that I was delivered from it.

That exercise of putting off and putting on prepared me for what was coming to test me. This test gave me the opportunity to either pass or fail.

The love of Christ took care of all my weaknesses and the weaknesses of others. After all, we can take hold of the truth that Jesus said, "Father forgive them for they know not what they do."

This takes away all of the excuses and allows us to love everyone, even in all of their weaknesses, and to follow Christ, allowing our deeds to be spoken well of. Hallelujah!!

Luke 23:34 (ESV): And Jesus said, "Father, forgive them, for they know not what they do." And they cast lots to divide his garments.

47

Jesus, a successful Author

The Spirit of the Lord said the most reassuring, comforting words to me. I was questioning myself whether I was going to succeed at being a writer.

I guess the unknown was getting the best of me and leaving me wondering if it was possible for my life to be changed in a way I knew nothing of.

I was stopped right in my tracks to hear the sweet voice of the Holy Spirit respond to my thoughts, "I am a Writer, I am a Publisher, I am a Marketer, and I AM Good Success!"

Taking hold of walking by faith and not by sight is not always easy to grasp. But I am learning that walking by faith is totally trusting and reaching out to Jesus for help and looking to Him for all the answers.

There is no need for me to know where I'm going when Jesus knows where I'm going, as long as it is His plan for me.

Hallelujah!!

Hebrews 11:8 (NLT): It was by faith that Abraham obeyed when God called him to leave home and go to another land that God would give him as his inheritance. He went without knowing where he was going.

48

Early morning truth responded

My husband and I had been preparing all week for one of the largest festivals in Marietta, Georgia. The people in charge of planning this festival estimated between one-hundred and two-hundred thousand people every year.

As my husband and I were preparing for this grand-scale festival, I noticed something had come over me that was making me uncomfortable participating in the festival. The closer the date came, the greater the fear rose up, which was becoming a struggle.

This overwhelming battle of nervousness I was experiencing was a challenge to shake off, and it was trying to get the best of me.

So I examined myself and asked, "What do we have here?" Then with a deliberate command, I responded to that nervousness, "Nervousness, I'm sending you away NOW, in the name of Jesus!"

The next morning, which was the first day of the festival, at about 1:28 a.m., my husband decides to read the Bible. I am lying down listening to him. I did not know, nor was my husband aware, what was about to happen.

As he was reading the Scripture, Jesus provided His Word of evidence to comfort me and to show me His love. A calmness came over me, assuring me that Jesus is my helper!"

Immediately, I knew that was from God. He was compassionately con-

soling me with His love and reassurance.
   Hallelujah!!

Hebrews 13:6 (NLT): So we can say with confidence, "The LORD is my helper, so I will have no fear. What can mere people do to me?"

49

Perfect way for our husbands

I was on my knees one day thanking the Lord when the Spirit of the Lord suddenly said, "Continue to be a witness for your husband, it is very important."

The Spirit of the Lord continued to tell me that my character and how I respond to things in the presence of my husband, will either encourage him to change or discourage him, causing him to struggle and making it impossible to change.

I believe this truth that was given to me was for my good as well as for my husband's good. The reason is because it helps us as wives to continue to examine ourselves to be pleasing to the Lord Jesus in our deeds. Certainly when we are pleasing to the Lord Jesus, we become a great example to our husbands.

Our spouses should see the character of Jesus in us, and our responses should be in line with the Word of God. Jesus always approaches his children with love that illuminates His Word. This is His glorious identification.

God is glorified in the highest, and He allows wives to be a witness, through the power of the Holy Ghost, to see Jesus and receive the way He loves. This wonderful exemplification of Jesus shows us the perfect picture of His eternal love.

The day before the Holy Spirit began showing me this, my husband had been disappointed about not getting any sales at his place of work. His conversation was unpleasant as he told me about his day. Although it was unpleasant to listen to, I realized I needed to stay quiet and not involve myself in his complaining.

A few minutes went by, and he settled down and began to get quiet. To my surprise, my husband started talking about something pleasant. What he did not know was that I had been praying under my breath when he was complaining. What I did not know was his conversation was going to shift right away to a pleasant one.

"Wow," I thought to myself, "talk about a quick response from God!" I had seen the glory of the Lord in action. My quietness and prayer had opened the door for Jesus to settle things for our good.

Jesus turned the whole situation around for His glory. I am grateful for the direction of the Holy Spirit telling me to be quiet in the middle of an unpleasant conversation. The Holy Spirit allowed me to see through my obedience. I was a witness for Christ toward my husband because of the end result Christ showed us both.

This is not one-sided. My husband has been a wonderful witness in Christ for me as well. He has been a great witness and influential in loving me during those times when I am unloving. There have been many times I was wrong, and he continually overlooks my faults and pillows me with love.

This is the character of Jesus I have always been able to see in my husband. Wives and husbands are witnesses before Christ toward each other every day. Will it be bad or good? Quietness and prayer when things are troubled allows Christ Jesus to turn everything for our good as we remember that Jesus is Lord!

Hallelujah!!

Matthew 5:48 **(NLT):** But you are to be perfect, even as your Father in heaven is perfect.

50

First Class information

Wow! What did You say? I was doing some chores around the house when, all of a sudden, my steps came to a halt. I knew it was time to listen to the Spirit of the Lord.

He repeated, "Twelve people will be buying blenders today." My reaction was, "What!? Thank you, Lord!" Raising my hands, I said, "Yes!"

I was like a little kid going to the playground. This is how I respond when Jesus is telling me good news, or even when He corrects me. Just knowing my husband was going to make twelve sales was exciting. What was fascinating about this was that my husband did not know the Spirit of the Lord had communicated the good news to me, and I did not tell him.

Right before my husband walked out of the store, he called me and said, "Angela, I sold twelve blenders today." I calmly replied, "I know you did." There was a big smile on my face. That is what you call "First Class information."

Proverbs 8:6, 32 (NLT): "Listen to me! For I have important things to tell you. Everything I say is right ... And so, my children, listen to me, for all who follow my ways are joyful."

51

God's directions are well lit

Why have you been seeking to live your own way? Many times, you are unaware of your independent thinking and that you are not acknowledging Me in all of your endeavors. You do not acknowledge Me in all your endeavors because they are your endeavors and not my plans. Your endeavors have led you into a selfish state of mind, leading you astray, causing you to be double-minded, thinking it is for My glory when, in fact, it is for your own glory.

I can not give you what you need when your life is producing double intentions. It does not reflect My will nor the plans I have for you. More importantly, you can not see Me when your mind is blurred and confused with your doubled-minded endeavors.

There is no blur, no confusion, and no darkness when you are acknowledging Me in the plans I have for you. My directions are clear, peaceful, and well lit. Your ways are assured when it is My way.

Remember, I AM the Way, the Truth, and the Life!

Psalm 33:11-12 (NASB): The counsel of the LORD stands forever, The plans of His heart from generation to generation. Blessed is the nation whose God is the LORD, The people whom He has chosen for His own inheritance.

James 1:8 (NLT): Their loyalty is divided between God and the world, and they are unstable in everything they do.

52

Choose a word, make it good

Look out! What words are you saying? Should my heart duck, or should it stand at attention?

When God spoke, you saw what was created, and He affirmed that it was "Good."

Can we speak the same way, or not? Guard your heart. If you are guarding your heart, that means you are careful of what you say, especially what you say to others.

Okay, now you are going to think about what you say, right?

There are so many lovely words Jesus has given us to choose from. Let us make the right choice. Choose today to make your life "Good!"

Genesis 1:31 (NLT): Then God looked over all he had made, and he saw that it was very good! And evening passed and morning came, marking the sixth day.

Proverbs 18:21 (CJB): The tongue has power over life and death; those who indulge it must eat its fruit.

53

My name carried my purpose

What do you do when you find out after many years who you are in Christ? One night, I stayed up late and decided to look at the meaning of names.

My son is having his first son, and I explained to him how important it is to know the meaning of a name before it is documented. This is something I did not take heed to when my son was born, but thank God, my son has a meaningful name he can live up to.

I knew the meaning of my name, *Angela*, was "angel of God," but for some reason, I never took it to heart. I never pondered on the meaning of my name, so I decided to examine the meaning.

I knew the names in the Bible meant something that carried out their character. I did not quite understand why I needed to know at this point in my life what would unfold by its meaning. But I believe God knew. His timing is forever perfect.

I believe at that very moment, it was important for me to gain understanding of His calling on my life. And, to my surprise, not only did I see that *Angela* meant, "angel of God," but I also saw that it meant, "messenger of God!" I must have gazed at the meaning for fifteen minutes.

My purpose jumped out at me! Suddenly, my mind took another direction. This meaning, "messenger of God," gave me direction, meaning, and purpose. I stopped and thought, *how could I not have known all this time that my name carried my purpose for Christ?*

God has given me a gift to encourage others in a way that they will listen. I love to encourage people in the Lord Jesus, telling them about His goodness.

Now, I have a clear pathway of living up to the meaning of my name through Christ Jesus, the name that was given me at my conception. I did not see it before, but I see it now! Hallelujah!

———————

Philippians 3:14 (ONM): I press on toward that goal, the prize that is the object of the upward call of God in Messiah Y'shua.

54

Know who I AM, and know who I am not

Reach out to Me! Seek Me! Run to Me! Get to know Me! When you draw unto Me, I will draw unto you. You will always be able to discern Who I Am, and who you are not when you seek Me.

The world will never be able to deceive you because of your knowledge of Me because you abide in Me and I in you.

Matthew 16:13-16 (NLT): When Jesus came to the region of Caesarea Philippi, he asked his disciples, "Who do people say that the Son of Man is?" "Well," they replied, "some say John the Baptist, some say Elijah, and others say Jeremiah or one of the other prophets." Then he asked them, "But who do you say I am?" Simon Peter answered, "You are the Messiah, the Son of the living God."

55

Follow fruitfulness, leave artificial food behind

Watch out! Many false prophets are leading God's people astray. They are being fed artificial food.

You may ask, "What is this artificial food?"

It is empty words, vain communication, and fruitless proclamations. What happens to a tree when it is fruitless? Well, we cannot eat from it, nor can we share it with others.

Likewise, when we are fed artificial food from false prophets, we are led to a deadend road that takes us nowhere.

Let us follow fruitfulness, which is in the Word of God, and listen to His voice with an exuberance of faith. This assures our destination, "believing the Way, the Truth and the Life in Christ Jesus!"

Hallelujah!

John 15:4 (NLT): Remain in me, and I will remain in you. For a branch cannot produce fruit if it is severed from the vine, and you cannot be fruitful unless you remain in me.

56

Let me put on the Holy Spirit Son glasses

I was rolling around in the dark trying to find my way, but my flesh would not let me see where I was going. I was opening my heart to the Lord and being honest about my situation and my weaknesses.

I said, "Lord, I'm writing this book You instructed me to write, but I do not have the finances to get it published nor to market it." I explained to the Lord that I just did not know how it was going to happen. I cannot do it, and I do not know how to do it.

The Spirit of the Lord used a true event in the Bible to convince me, so that I would understand the way He does things. And would not you know it, He used one of my favorite events in the Bible, the story of Jehoshaphat.

When Jehoshaphat heard about the armies coming against him, he was afraid. He did not know what to do. Jehoshaphat did the most effective thing he could do. He prayed, and he told the Lord he was afraid. He was very honest. We do not have to pretend we're not afraid or that we do not know what to do. You see when Jehoshaphat went to the Lord in honesty of his fear, it was because he trusted the Lord and not himself.

Because of Jehoshaphat's trust in the Lord, something miraculous happened. The Lord gave Jehoshaphat instructions of what to do. Those instructions from the Lord gave him confidence to do them.

The Lord did not tell Jehoshaphat everything all that once that was going to happened. What Jehoshaphat was assured of was that God gave him confidence to move forward with what was revealed to him at that moment.

The Holy Spirit said, "Angela, you do not have to know everything all at once. Go with what I have given you, and then you will see the rest when you get there. As long as you are in my plan, everything has already been established for you."

---

2 Chronicles 20:3-26 (NLT): 3 Jehoshaphat was terrified by this news and begged the Lord for guidance. He also ordered everyone in Judah to begin fasting.
4 So people from all the towns of Judah came to Jerusalem to seek the Lord's help.
5 Jehoshaphat stood before the community of Judah and Jerusalem in front of the new courtyard at the Temple of the Lord.
6 He prayed, "O Lord, God of our ancestors, you alone are the God who is in heaven. You are ruler of all the kingdoms of the earth. You are powerful and mighty; no one can stand against you!
7 O our God, did you not drive out those who lived in this land when your people Israel arrived? And did you not give this land forever to the descendants of your friend Abraham?
8 Your people settled here and built this Temple to honor your name.
9 They said, 'Whenever we are faced with any calamity such as war, plague, or famine, we can come to stand in your presence before this Temple where your name is honored. We can cry out to you to save us, and you will hear us and rescue us.'
10 "And now see what the armies of Ammon, Moab, and Mount Seir are doing. You would not let our ancestors invade those nations when Israel left Egypt, so they went around them and did not destroy them.
11 Now see how they reward us! For they have come to throw us out of your land, which you gave us as an inheritance.
12 O our God, won't you stop them? We are powerless against this mighty army that is about to attack us. We do not know what to do, but we are looking to you

for help."

13 As all the men of Judah stood before the Lord with their little ones, wives, and children,

14 the Spirit of the Lord came upon one of the men standing there. His name was Jahaziel son of Zechariah, son of Benaiah, son of Jeiel, son of Mattaniah, a Levite who was a descendant of Asaph.

15 He said, "Listen, all you people of Judah and Jerusalem! Listen, King Jehoshaphat! This is what the Lord says: Do not be afraid! Don't be discouraged by this mighty army, for the battle is not yours, but God's.

16 Tomorrow, march out against them. You will find them coming up through the ascent of Ziz at the end of the valley that opens into the wilderness of Jeruel.

17 But you will not even need to fight. Take your positions; then stand still and watch the Lord's victory. He is with you, O people of Judah and Jerusalem. Do not be afraid or discouraged. Go out against them tomorrow, for the Lord is with you!"

18 Then King Jehoshaphat bowed low with his face to the ground. And all the people of Judah and Jerusalem did the same, worshiping the Lord.

19 Then the Levites from the clans of Kohath and Korah stood to praise the Lord, the God of Israel, with a very loud shout.

20 Early the next morning the army of Judah went out into the wilderness of Tekoa. On the way Jehoshaphat stopped and said, "Listen to me, all you people of Judah and Jerusalem! Believe in the Lord your God, and you will be able to stand firm. Believe in his prophets, and you will succeed."

21 After consulting the people, the king appointed singers to walk ahead of the army, singing to the Lord and praising him for his holy splendor. This is what they sang: "Give thanks to the Lord; his faithful love endures forever!"

22 At the very moment they began to sing and give praise, the Lord caused the armies of Ammon, Moab, and Mount Seir to start fighting among themselves.

23 The armies of Moab and Ammon turned against their allies from Mount Seir and killed every one of them. After they had destroyed the army of Seir, they began attacking each other.

24 So when the army of Judah arrived at the lookout point in the wilderness, all they saw were dead bodies lying on the ground as far as they could see. Not a single one of the enemy had escaped.

25 King Jehoshaphat and his men went out to gather the plunder. They found vast amounts of equipment, clothing, and other valuables—more than they could carry. There was so much plunder that it took them three days just to collect it all!
26 On the fourth day they gathered in the Valley of Blessing, which got its name that day because the people praised and thanked the Lord there. It is still called the Valley of Blessing today.

57

Memory Lane not worth remembering

I was speaking in my heavenly language when I suddenly felt an unction to stop and listen. The Spirit of the Lord made me aware of the reason why I felt bothered by observing pictures taken from my past.

He made it clear that the reason I was feeling an uneasiness was because I was not in Him at that time. Those pictures were pictures of my past when Christ Jesus had no involvement in my life. They reflected when my heart was far from Him.

The more I reviewed those pictures, the deeper my mind was absorbing the memories that took place, drawing fine print images of which I did not care to be reminded.

At that very hour, it was revealed to me that when you have a relationship with Christ, your spirit picks up messages and signals warning you of things not pleasing to Him. So when I felt uneasiness, it was when correction was taking place to remind me of who I am in Jesus Christ today.

The Spirit of the Lord cautioned me not to go back into the review mirror of my past.

Some of the pictures that reflected my past brought conviction as though I was still involved in those things, although I was not. Being awakened to the truth, I knew I had to forget those things that were behind and press on toward the One Who is the head of my life now, Christ Jesus.

A lesson was learned in this particular situation: leave all things behind, that do not involve Christ Jesus.

Isaiah 43:18 (NASB): "Do not call to mind the former things, Or ponder things of the past ..."

1 Corinthians 2:2 (NASB): For I determined to know nothing among you except Jesus Christ, and Him crucified.

58

Love keeps us waiting for His coming

*L*et us always reflect on how we're able to see the salvation of the Lord and how our lives are changed because of it.

I have had many experiences of Jesus' love that keeps me drawn to Him and wanting to please Him. The ending results of believing the salvation of the Lord in my life is the most loving action that has ever taken place on earth.

Yes, His death, burial, and resurrection, were actions of love. I sometimes stop and think about how Jesus keeps every organ in our bodies functioning night and day. Believe it, when you wake up every morning, Jesus planned it that way, which is why we should inquire, "Lord, today, how can I please you?" I am thankful for Jesus always demonstrating His love that keeps us.

Hallelujah!

Daniel 6:27 (NLT): He rescues and saves his people; he performs miraculous signs and wonders in the heavens and on earth. He has rescued Daniel from the power of the lions. Waiting for His coming!

59

Come, get on the fantastic voyage

My stamp of approval was given to you when you became righteous through My death, burial, and resurrection. Your diligent work has shown the world who I AM. You have convinced them of the Salvation I have given freely. Now, they want to follow Me and share the same freedom they themselves saw in you. Come! Get on this fantastic voyage. It is free!

Hallelujah!

Daniel 6:27 (NLT): He rescues and saves his people; he performs miraculous signs and wonders in the heavens and on earth. He has rescued Daniel from the power of the lions.

60

A free ride settled by Jesus

It was so heavy on my mind to see my grandbaby, Pearl, who lives in Florida, before the end of the year 2013. For some reason, I felt like I needed to tell her and assure her that I will always love her.

As time was getting closer toward the end of the year, it did not seem like I would be able to see her. Neither finances nor time seemed like they would allow us to accomplish this desire.

Then something spectacular happened, and I did not realize it until I arrived home from the trip. My aunt, Anita, lives in Florida, and another aunt named Anna picked her up from there to spend time with us at our home in Atlanta for Thanksgiving.

The original plan was that Aunt Anna was going to take Aunt Anita back to Florida, but it did not work out that way.

Sometimes, we cannot see that God has worked things out in advance for what we have been asking for in our hearts. Plans changed, and I did not know they had changed to my favor from my Heavenly Father.

My cousin, Trina, asked me to ask my husband, Elliott, if we could help her with driving Aunt Anita back to Florida? I did not mind at all, but I did ask her if we could see our grandbaby, Pearl, while we were there, and she agreed. I asked my husband, and we agreed to do it.

She said we did not have to pay anything because she just needed help with the driving. At this point, it still did not occur to me that the Lord Jesus was giving me my heart's desire to see my grandbaby in Florida.

So we all made plans to go to Florida for a day and leave the very next morning. We arrived in Florida about 8:30 p.m. that evening and dropped my aunt off at her home. We told her we would be back.

I called my grandbaby's mom, Kate, and told her we were on our way there to see them. She was delighted to hear that we would be there in 30 to 40 minutes! I told her not to tell Pearl we would be there until we walk in the door.

When we arrived, Kate answered the door, greeting us with kisses and hugs, and asked us to sit in the living room because our grandbaby was upstairs. Kate called Pearl to come down. When she saw me, she gave me the longest, most loving hug, almost like a hug of something that had been lifted off her shoulder. She did not want me out of her sight.

Pearl took me to her bedroom and laid across my lap, as always, and started saying, "Grandmother, remember when you would let me stay up for a long time and we would talk?" My grandbaby was actually reminiscing of the good times we have had over so many years.

After she finished, I told her I will always love her, and Jesus will always love her with an everlasting love. Then, I popped the question I always asked her.

"What do you say whenever you're in trouble, or whenever someone hurts you, or whenever you're feeling sad? What do you say?"

She paused for a couple of minutes. I was surprised because she usually came right out with it. She could not remember, so I reminded her, "Jesus, help me!"

She responded, "Oh, yeah!"

I believe this trip was decided upon in Heaven because the Lord Jesus knew I had something of importance to say to my granddaughter face to face in remembrance of Him. I have been teaching her since she was three years old that whenever she experiences trouble, to ask Jesus to help her. It is of value and shows her the love Jesus has for her.

Our grandbaby is nine years old now at the time of this writing and has been saying, "Jesus, help me," since she was three years old. She has had the privilege of calling on His name whenever she was not feeling well, no matter the need.

God worked it all out, and my prayer was answered that I be allowed to see my grandbaby, Pearl, before the end of the year, at no charge!

Thank you Jesus for your faithfulness!

Hallelujah!

Psalms 54:4 (NIV): Surely God is my helper; the Lord is the One Who sustains me.

61

Stop your plans. Ask for Mine.

Whether I realize it or not, at times, I make plans without consulting with God. Then, after I have made the plans, I stop and ask myself if this is the plan of God. It is like going forward with my own plans without giving a thought to how my own plans are in vain if they are not the plans of God.

At that point, I have to halt, examine myself, and think about what I am doing without the counsel of God. After careful pondering, I realize that my anxious thoughts sometimes lead me to making plans without considering God's plan.

I have to quickly switch gears, repent, and ask God what plans He has for me. Asking God for His plans daily keeps me attentive to His voice by remembering that Jesus is the Way, the Truth, and Life. After careful examination and repenting for my disobedience, I hear the Spirit of the Lord say, "You are not your own."

Right away, I embraced His voice because Jesus said He corrects those He loves. What a timely correction to remind me of His love, making me aware that I live, move, and have my being in Him alone.

Proverbs 19:21 (NIV): Many are the plans in a person's heart, but it is the LORD's purpose that prevails

62

Never bow. Stand.

Shadrach, Meshach, and Abednego did not run from their jobs just because the king demanded something they did not believe, nor were they going to give in to it.

They were working for a king who believed in idolatry. They believed in their God, but they did not quit their jobs because the king had a different belief from theirs. Neither did they run when the king wanted them to believe and bow down to his gods. With boldness and trust in their God, they did not quit working for the king.

That story taught me that I do not have to quit my job because things may not go the way I would like. Perhaps someone might see the salvation of the Lord because of my staying there in boldness and not running every time something happens on the job.

Nebuchadnezzar was able to see the salvation of the Lord that Shadrach, Meshach, and Abednego trusted in. Nebuchadnezzar witnessed Shadrach, Meshach, and Abednego not being burnt from the fire, and he saw a fourth man, who was God, being with them in that furnace. Because of that witness, his heart was totally changed to believing in their God.

My point is this: stop running and quitting jobs because things do not go your way. Stand strong in God for what He is for and against. If you should one day have to go into the fire, God will surely bring you out of the fire, and you and others shall see the salvation of the Lord, as did Nebuchadnezzar.

Hallelujah!

Daniel 3:16-18 (NLT): Shadrach, Meshach, and Abednego replied, "O Nebuchadnezzar, we do not need to defend ourselves before you. If we are thrown into the blazing furnace, the God whom we serve is able to save us. He will rescue us from your power, Your Majesty. But even if he doesn't, we want to make it clear to you, Your Majesty, that we will never serve your gods or worship the gold statue you have set up."

63

Morning word makes our days brighter

In a world where there are so many distractions, one has to consciously keep their mind stayed on Jesus. This is a choice we must make every day, whether it is conscious or unconscious.

Every morning, I take the liberty wholeheartedly to say when I wake up, "Lord, wake up my ears to hear what you have to say." Then I thank Him for waking up my ears to hear Him.

To listen to the revelation of the Lord in the mornings is the most precious and needful instruction you can ever receive. We are talking about a loving Father speaking through His Son, Jesus, Who sits on the throne and gives us a personal, loving Word, whether it is instruction, correction, or encouragement.

Whatever His Word is, it is for our good for the day. Oh, how sweet it is to listen to a trusted Father Who loves us with an everlasting love.

You know when you receive either instruction or encouragement (both are comforting), your day is inspired to withstand anything that comes your way. The Spirit's morning Word sets up your day with peace that you can meditate on all throughout the day. And if anything arises, reflecting on His Word is like the brightness of the sun. Receiving God's Word in the mornings makes our days brighter.

Hallelujah!

Isaiah 50:4 (NLT): The Sovereign LORD has given me his words of wisdom, so that I know how to comfort the weary. Morning by morning he wakens me and opens my understanding to his will.

64

Speak good fruit

I noticed something had changed in me the previous two weeks. I had been cranky, and complaining about every little thing. What had gotten in to me? That is my point.

I had been working more hours because we were short of manpower that I had been very tired. On a daily basis, when I get home or before I go to work, the Holy Spirit and I commune with one another. I absolutely love being in the presence of the Holy Spirit. He shares great wisdom with me for my good and for the good of others to share.

Lack of being in His presence gave room for me to turn my attention to myself, which led to complaining about everything around me. Spoiled fruit was coming out of my mouth and surrounding me with unhappiness. It was also affecting those around me, as well.

Then one late night after leaving work and arriving home, I was determined I was going to spend some time with the One I love to be with: the Holy Spirit. He lovingly said to me, "Angela, your flesh can never please Me. When you complain and murmur, you only have yourself in mind. You have totally turned from Me, just like the children of Israel.

"Your words are speaking of your inconveniences and displeasures. Speaking complaints and inconveniences will never declare My Truth, and no one will be able to see My Truth and benefit from it. What happened to My Word that gives life? What happened to you being thankful in all things? Let only My Word be declared in your mouth! Out of your mouth, only let My Word speak truth! Speak only the good fruit of My Spirit! It is My Word I want people to see and perform, not your vain words! Repent!"

Hallelujah!!!

Psalm 119:172 (KJV): My tongue shall speak of thy word: for all thy commandments *are* righteousness.

1 John 1:1 (ONM): The One Who was from the beginning, Whom we have heard, Whom we have seen with our eyes, Whom we looked upon and our hands touched concerning the very Word of Life.

65

Trust God searching for unfamiliar work

Looking for work has been a job in itself. Then I began to review my whole outlook in seeking work to do.

In my search for employment, I asked myself if I should look for work I'm familiar with but that would not require faith. Well, that would leave me with something I should be doing from the start, walking by faith.

So I decided to trust God in my search for employment and make no room for the flesh to get weary. I started applying for work I had never done before. Keeping God's promise in mind, I am walking by faith and not by sight.

I knew keeping this promise in mind would not leave any room for reasoning. Even if it meant me not making as much money as I would like, I knew something bigger than myself would manifest, and I would not be able to take glory for it. My Lord Jesus Christ would get all the glory.

I realized how beautiful it is to seek work from a Savior Who knows about everything because He created the heavens, the earth, and everything in it. Keeping this in mind assured me that whatever door of employment God opened for me, He surely has already given me the ability to accomplish it. Therefore is there anything too hard for God? Absolutely not!

He created all things for His glory. Trusting in my Father for work I have never done but can do with His strength and help is His promise.

Now I am doing something I have never thought of doing. I am trusting God for doing something unfamiliar and allowed me to look unto Him for help. After all, He is my Helper.

Seeing the salvation of the Lord gives me the opportunity to give Him glory and testify of His goodness and faithfulness.

Hallelujah!

Colossians 1:16 (NLT): ... for through him God created everything in the heavenly realms and on earth. He made the things we can see and the things we can't see-- such as thrones, kingdoms, rulers, and authorities in the unseen world. Everything was created through him and for him.

66

Testimonies bring our listeners to the feet of Jesus

A good friend of mine named John reported news from the doctor that greatly put him in a state of shock and fear. As I listened to John tell about what the doctor disclosed, my first instinct was to read the Scriptures to him. But then a whisper came to me, "A better way to convince John of Jesus' love for him in this very situation is for John to know that God knew about his situation before he was in his mother's womb."

John needed to know that God, the Creator of heaven and earth and everything in it, knows everything beforehand and is not caught off guard by anything. From John's conversation, he could not see anything past his discomfort and fear of the doctor's diagnosis.

I immediate knew John's thoughts needed to be changed quickly and that he needed to be influenced by testimonies of Jesus' love and faithfulness.

This gave me the opportunity to give God glory and honor in sharing testimonies with John to make him aware that God has not left him nor forsaken him.

After sharing my testimonies that led me to see the salvation of the Lord, I prayed that John would be inspired by God's love and kindness and that, with this mindset, it would lead him to God's peace.

After sharing my testimonies, John thanked me as if his spirit had been quieted. I realized the best way to comfort John was to share my testimonies of the goodness of Christ Jesus Who is definitely the Hope of Glory. These testimonies of seeing the salvation of the Lord put John's mind at ease and convinced him that he does not have to look at the problem. Jesus had already overcame what he was experiencing.

I shared with John that I witnessed my trials turning into triumphs. Sharing my testimonies seem to capture John's mind with amazement but with comfort, enabling him to breathe with assurance that our heavenly Father is always with us, no matter what the cause.

Sharing our testimonies with others brings our listeners to the feet of Jesus to see His miraculous works upon the earth, and that He is still operating in the earth today. A bad report in the eyes of man can be a good report in the eyes of Jesus.

You may ask how this could be. Well, sometimes, we look at reports from the doctor that do not seem fair as being bad reports. However, once we search out God's truth to see what He has to say about the situation, then the light that seemed so dim shows us His bright light that explains His love and kindness in every situation when we choose to look at His benefits and promises.

Hallelujah!

Isaiah 52:7 (NLT): How beautiful on the mountains are the feet of the messenger who brings good news, the good news of peace and salvation, the news that the God of Israel reigns!

67

Now, go, Angela.
I AM is with your mouth!

Go! I will be with your mouth, said the Spirit of the Lord. I was preparing for an interview, and I did not feel comfortable because it had been a while since I had been on an interview.

My desire was to be able to answer all interview questions to their satisfaction in order to get the job. So I started searching the internet for interview questions for that field of employment.

After reviewing and preparing how I was going to respond to the questions, the Holy Spirit intervened with love, as always, and took me to Exodus 4:12. He said emphatically, "NOW GO! I AM will be with your mouth, and I will teach you what you will say."

As I was reading and meditating on this truth given to me, I suddenly began to experience confidence and assurance of God's Word, not knowing exactly what was going to happen as a result of obeying it. Although I was meditating on God's truth, my flesh wanted to continue to prepare my own way for the interview. The Spirit of the Lord said, "Stop! I will tell you what to say."

I stopped instantly, being reminded of how important it is to obey the voice of the Lord. With absolutely no more hesitation, I was determined I would trust the Lord with all my heart concerning the interview.

As I studied the Word and meditated, I began to see and understand why God put His Word in Moses' mouth. God accomplishes His purpose with His Word so He would be glorified. This truth led me to review other Scriptures where God put His Word in others, and they took heed to His instructions that resulted in miraculous works.

Wow, the more I read, the more my faith was being built up and prepared for what I was about to see. Oh, how my heart pitter-pattered with belief because I knew something was about to happen that I had never seen before. God's chosen Word assured me that He was with me, and I had nothing to fear. All doubts had diminished.

I no longer looked at my weaknesses but stared straight ahead at the Lord Himself through His Word. I was completely inspired by His firm instructions, believing that He is the same as He was back then during Moses' day.

I woke up the next morning, the day of my interview, completely zealous and holding on to the Word, "Now Go!" I will be with your mouth.

I arrived at the place of the interview, and two people named Jack and Sheila came out to interview me at the same time. They started firing questions and like never before, my answers were not from me but definitely from the Lord. I could not have thought of the answers I gave.

Jack and Sheila said they enjoyed the interview and that they had never heard some of my answers communicated that way. Jack said he liked my personality so much that he wanted someone in another department named Vic to interview me before I left. What Jack did not know is that Vic's department is where I originally wanted to work.

Vic, from my desired department, approach me, and as he introduced himself to me, I knew when I opened my mouth, the Lord was with my mouth as I was speaking to him. As I answered Vic's questions, his response was, "I really like you."

After the interview ended, Vic said he wanted someone named Patricia from the same department to interview me and that she would give me a call to set up another interview. As I was walking out the door toward my car, I started praising the Lord, amazed at how He spoke every word through my mouth, giving me favor with my interviewers.

Before interviewing with Patricia, the Spirit of the Lord told me when she asked me if I had any questions to respond, "Will you give me the job?" When I asked Patricia this question, she laughed and said, "I wish I could, but unfortunately, I'm not the one who hires."

After the interview ended, she said she would set an appointment for me to interview with the store manager named Jesse. Again, the Spirit of the Lord gave me instructions to respond, "Will you give me the job?" when Jesse asked if I had any questions. Jesse interviewed me for about five minutes and asked if I had any questions. Of course, I obeyed my Father's instructions and responded, "Will you give me the job?" Jesse laughed and said, "We'll get your schedule set up."

It was the first time I had ever been aware of Jesus speaking through my mouth. The Spirit of the Lord had full control. I am convinced that my body belongs to the Lord. Everything worked in my favor all because of what the Lord put in my mouth to say, and I obeyed.

It definitely worked out for my good because Jesus put me in the department where I desired to work. How did it happened? It was miraculous! This experience will forever be a documented testimony in my heart.

Hallelujah!

Exodus 4:12 (NLT): "… Now go! I will be with you as you speak, and I will instruct you in what to say."

Revelation 3:8 (NASB): "… 'I know your deeds. Behold, I have put before you an open door which no one can shut, because you have a little power, and have kept My word, and have not denied My name…'"

68

A wink brought laughter

Elizabeth is another one of my grandbabies who captures your attention with her beautiful big bright eyes. You can take Elizabeth anywhere, and people will stop and compliment her big bright eyes.

In the summer of 2013, my husband and I had both grandchildren staying with us. I had cooked breakfast, and my oldest granddaughter, Pearl, had finished and excused herself from the table. My next to the youngest granddaughter, Elizabeth, was still finishing her breakfast.

Although Elizabeth is very small, she is a big eater and will ask for more several times. One thing I noticed about Elizabeth is that it does not bother her to be left alone at the table as long as she can get more food.

After she finishes her first plate, she loves to say, "Grandmother, may I please have some more?" I put my hands on my hips and say with a smile, "Little girl, no more for you," and both of us burst out laughing.

Well, this same morning, Elizabeth made the sweetest gesture I have ever seen from a three-year-old.

As I was washing the dishes and keeping a close watch on Elizabeth at the table until she finished her breakfast, Elizabeth unexpectedly gazed at me, gave me a big smile, and a long wink. My mouth flew wide open and out came a hearty laugh. I was amazed that she was able to wink as though she knew what she was doing.

I must say, I had never seen anything like that from a three-year-old.

I ran over to her, grabbed her in my arms, and gave her the biggest hug and kiss. we both were laughing. When I put Elizabeth down, I shook my head because she had made my day as bright as her eyes are bright.

Hallelujah!

Genesis 21:6 (NLT): And Sarah declared, "God has brought me laughter. All who hear about this will laugh with me..."

69

Move and finish

My ears were awakened this particular morning with a special word from the Spirit of the Lord commanding me to "Finish." Jesus knows my heart, and He knew there was a hesitance in me about moving forward to finish this book. I knew immediately what it was about and that my faith had to increase and be taken to another level.

Whenever it was time to sit down and continue typing the book, I would look at the chair and wonder, *will I be able to finish?* When I heard the Spirit of the Lord's command to finish it, it gave me confidence. I knew from then on that I could do it with His help. After all, it is written in His Word "God is my helper."

God's affirming Word gave me boldness to run to the finish line with no hesitancy or fear. Now when I sit down to type my book, I know it is in His will for me to complete it because His Words flow freely in me.

Also, God's Word revealed that He is doing a new thing in me for His glory that will be seen in all the earth. I know it is extremely important that His will be done here on earth through me. Like never before, I am focusing on finishing this book with the strength God has given me, not allowing any stumbling blocks to stop me.

God's positive Word to finish requires me to hold on to His righteous right hand and not let go. My sight had to be blinded to be able to hear what the Spirit of the Lord was commanding me to do. Therefore, the Spirit illuminated my heart and set me on the right path to finish the plans He has for me because He is doing a new thing in me.

Hallelujah!

Isaiah 43:19 (NASB): "Behold, I will do something new, now it will spring forth; will you not be aware of it? I will even make a roadway in the wilderness, rivers in the desert..."

70

Your heart from God's point of view

Why did I not know this sooner? Sometimes it takes the heart time to develop and understand situations. And the most fascinating part about understanding your heart is that you are not aware it is changing and becoming more pure because of your relationship with Jesus.

Gradually, I began to notice that I wanted so deeply to please my heavenly Father. I began to examine myself often, making sure my deeds were right in His sight, and if not, I repented quickly.

All of my heartfelt need to please God came with meditating on His goodness and how He has rescued us time and time again. I take it serious that Jesus is all knowing, and nothing can be hidden from Him, so why try. God encourages me to be honest with myself and Him. God allows me to have a perfect relationship with Him because, when I fall short, I can lovingly face Him to repent and continue to move forward with pleasing Him.

As I mediated on His Word, I began to realize my heart was becoming sensitive to His will. I knew this because I experienced tests of where the heart is and what shape it is in. These tests take place at different times and places—the work place, with family members, etc. It can show up anywhere.

God has a way of showing us where we are through our heart. Sometimes it is encouraging, and sometimes it is disappointing. Either way, we can always ask the Holy Spirit to help us and show us the truth in God's Word.

This purification of heart through meditating and acting on the Word continues to change my heart regarding situations that deeply matter to God. Keep in mind that we are responsible for keeping up with our own maintenance. Ensuring that our own heart is right with God is of the upmost of importance in pleasing Him.

Hallelujah!

Acts 1:24 (ONM): And when they prayed they said, "You Lord, because You know the hearts of all, show clearly whom You chose, one from these two …"

71

Downloading the Word of God

A challenge opened an opportunity for God to show His glory. My heart sank when I looked at the schedule at my new job and saw that I would be opening the store in the morning for the first time. That meant that I would be there by myself for the first two and one-half hours until the next employee came in.

I was taken aback. Immediately, fear tried to speak, saying, "How are you going to do that? You've never done this before." That voice of fear kept trying to put scary doubts in my mind. It tried to get me to succumb and bow down to its tactics to accomplish its purpose.

There were certain tasks that had to be done within a 30 minutes time frame before customers entered the store. As I was working, that voice of fear was trying to make me look foolish and incompetent in my abilities to do what I was instructed to do.

Then I paused, purposely put my thoughts into another gear, and started downloading the Word of God, reminding myself that God is my Perfect Peace, my Spirit of Truth, and my Salvation. I knew the downloading of God's Word into my thoughts was a shield that could not be penetrated. As I meditated on the Word of Truth while working that morning, I felt like the Spirit of Truth was carrying me, as if those duties were being done for me.

I had asked the Holy Spirit to help me, but before I asked Him to help me, I wanted to throw my hands up and run away from the situation. Then a sweet voice from the Spirit of the Lord asked me, "How am I going to help you if I do not open up opportunities to do so? This is the only way you and others will see My glory manifested. I AM is glorified by opening opportunities that are impossible for you, but possible with Me."

Then, the Spirit of the Lord affirmed a truth that stopped me in my tracks and transformed my mind. "Welcome and expect opportunities to happen, so you will always see my manifested glory. These opportunities that are impossible with man but possible with Me caused others to believe and follow Me."

I stood up straight with a big smile on my face knowing I had just deposited a gold nugget in my heart that will continue to sustain me forever. Understanding impossibilities allows me the opportunity to see the salvation of the Lord and not be ashamed of my own weaknesses.

For when I am weak, then I am strong. This is something to boast about and a way to bring others to Christ. This means I must go and not fold up in fear, "go to see the salvation of the Lord." Now, I no longer have to fear things that are impossible for me. I simply embrace the opportunity to see His strength and salvation manifesting through Christ in the earth.

Hallelujah!

---

2 Corinthians 12:9 (NLT): Each time he said, "My grace is all you need. My power works best in weakness." So now I am glad to boast about my weaknesses, so that the power of Christ can work through me.

72

Be ready for your Bridegroom

I woke up one morning expecting to receive my paycheck in the mail. I had been patiently waiting for my first check for about two and a half months and still had not received it.

Was there a problem with the postal service? Or was the company showing no interest in my receiving my first check I had worked hard for? No one seemed to be able to figure out what had happened to my paycheck. And from my point of view, it did not appear to me that they were concerned about how my not having this check inconvenienced my personal affairs.

My co-workers had already received three checks, and I was still waiting for my first one. Every morning, I got up early expecting my check to be in the mailbox only to be disappointed when I did not find anything in the mailbox or hear a knock at the door.

As I was waiting for my check to show up at my door, the Spirit of the Lord lovingly spoke as I was putting on my clothes, "You know how you got up this morning, dressed yourself, and made yourself ready to receive the check? Without a doubt you were expecting it to show up, expecting that knock on the door from the postman. You even said to yourself, 'I'm going to make sure I'm up early, so I do not miss the knock at the door.'

"The reason you wanted to get up early, be dressed, and ready for the postman is because of what happened in the past. You did not hear the postman knock at the door, and you missed receiving the package. Therefore, you did not want to miss the postman to receive your check. Likewise," the Spirit of the Lord said, "I want you to be purposefully and intentionally ready for Me, your Bridegroom, at every second because I can come at any time. And if you are always ready, then you do not have to be worried about the time when I will be there. Expect Me to come. Be ready!"

Suddenly, my waiting on my check had caused me to hear from the Lord. He turned my frustration into joy. I did receive my check that day, but hearing from the Spirit of the Lord, Who is my Counselor, gave me great peace through His instructions. Hallelujah!

Matthew 24:44 (NASB): For this reason you also must be ready; for the Son of Man is coming at an hour when you do not think He will.

73

Pleasing Jesus has become my affection

It was a beautiful sunny day, and I was returning home from Florida. I decided to ask the Lord directly if my writing and having a book published would be pleasing to Him.

In my mind, I was thinking that I wanted to give myself to Him as a living sacrifice, holy and acceptable, and nothing less. This deep thought had to be settled right there before I went any farther.

I asked the Spirit of the Lord if my wanting to be a published author would be pleasing to Him. The Spirit of the Lord responded, "In your writings, you are praising Me, you are thanking Me, you are exalting My name, you are acknowledging Me. You are doing what I desire—giving Me glory! Yes, you are pleasing Me!"

With a deeply inhaled relief and a burst of joy and peace, I thought to myself how comforting it is to get a confirmed blessing directly from the Spirit of God.

Therefore, I am moving forward, pressing toward the goal that has been set before me. Hallelujah!

Psalm 57:7 (KJV): My heart is fixed, O God, my heart is fixed: I will sing and give praise.

74

A monumental word

As I was enjoying my Bible study, a particular Scripture caught my attention. I felt I needed to meditate on it and get a deeper understanding of it. The Spirit of the Lord was telling me that no matter what is happening, good or bad, to give Him thanks.

I had no idea why it was necessary for me to know this right at this moment, but I took it to heart because it was a Word from the Lord. I was receiving revelation on this particular verse as though it was preparing me for something, but I did not know for what.

Then it happened the following day. I was on the road, coming back from an interview. I decided to stop by the grocery store, and my cousin Trina called. I waited until I was parked in the parking lot of the supermarket before calling her back.

I could not believe what I was hearing. Shocked and in disbelief, I heard Trina say the paramedics were there for my mother. My mother told Trina that her heart was beating hard and fast, and she felt severe pain. So they called the paramedics.

I wanted to talk to my mother, but I could not because she was with the paramedics. I asked Trina if she knew what was going on, and she said no. She said she would call me back. I did not want to get off the phone, but I knew she needed to find out what was going on.

I rushed home to pack my clothes. On my way home, I started praising and thanking the Lord, not even thinking about the Scripture that had jumped out at me the night before.

I arrived home, dropped my things, and continued thanking the Lord. The tears started rolling down my face, but it was not out of fear. I felt a shield of comfort and peace that definitely surpassed my understanding.

I called my Uncle Brent, my mom's brother, to inform him of the situation. I wanted to rush over to be with my mom, but I could not because my husband and I were working out of one vehicle, and my husband was due to be off work in an hour.

I packed my things, but, as I was packing, I was still thanking and praising the Lord for all of His goodness and His everlasting love. I did not mention anything about my mother. Then I walked out the door and got in my car to go pick up my husband, but before arriving at my husband's work site, I called my Aunt Anita who lives in Florida. My Aunt Anita had already been notified of my mom's situation by my cousin Trina. We started thanking and worshiping the Lord. During our worship, my Aunt Anita said she saw my mother sitting up and laughing in the hospital room. We started thanking God for what Aunt Anita saw in the Spirit.

I felt my flesh wanting to go out of control, but the Spirit of God overtook my mind and kept my body in perfect peace. I felt like fear was trying to get through but could not because of our thankfulness and praises to our Lord Jesus.

The Scripture that was given to me the night before by the Holy Spirit dominated my being and reminded and instructed me what I needed to continue to do. That was to continue to thank Him in all circumstances.

As I kept thanking God, a shield of protection took over, keeping fear from entering into my mind and sealing it with joy, comfort, and the assurance of Jesus' love. It felt like we were being closely guarded from fear and surrounded by a peace that can not be explained. I was so comforted with peace by the Holy Spirit that I did not feel rushed to be with my mother because I knew Jesus was with her.

My Aunt Anita and I ended our call with joy and confidence that we would see my mother. By that time, I was at my husband Elliott's work site to pick him up. I informed Elliott what had happened. When I called Trina to see where my mom was, she said they had taken her to the hospital.

My husband and I headed to the hospital, but when we got there, one of the hospital staff said she had been there, but they had taken her to another hospital. So we started driving toward the other hospital. As my husband and I were approaching the hospital, one of the doctors called me saying they had almost lost my mom on the way to the hospital. She had stopped breathing. The doctor also said my mom's heart had stopped again on the emergency table, but they were able to get it going again. They had to do an emergency surgery on her heart.

After being told all of this, fear still did not have a chance because my heart was so filled with thankfulness. My conscience was saying that all of this had happened to my mom, and I had not even seen her yet. But the truth was that although I had not seen my mom, God had, and He is sufficient for my mother and me.

I kept praising the Lord because I realized this was happening at the same time my Aunt Anita and I had been praising and worshiping the Lord.

When we arrived at the hospital, they had just finished surgery and said it was successful. They said we could see my mother in about 30 minutes. When we were approaching her room, my mom was slightly reclined and laughing and talking as though nothing had happened to her. It was just like what my Aunt Anita had seen through our thanksgiving and worship of God.

I called my Aunt Anita on the phone, and she shouted over and over again, "Praise the Lord!" We were all rejoicing in the Lord's goodness, faithfulness, and His miraculous work that He so lovingly had shown us.

I left my mother's room with tears of joy and went somewhere alone to thank the Lord in private for His faithfulness. He had restored life to my mother. The Spirit of the Lord brought back to my memory the Scripture to thank Him in all circumstances not knowing that I would see the salvation of the Lord. Seeing the Lord and His magnificence in this situation will forever be remembered monumentally in my heart.

Hallelujah!

---

1 Thessalonians 5:18 (NLT): Be thankful in all circumstances, for this is God's will for you who belong to Christ Jesus.

75

Rain held for my safety

I was concerned about the weather, so I decided to look at the five-day forecast for Atlanta. It was forecasted that we would have a seventy percent chance of rain that night.

I was thinking that the projected rain would be at the same time I would be on my way home from work. And the trip home was not necessarily short. Driving in the rain at night is a challenge. Therefore, the drive is uncomfortable at times, depending on how hard it's raining. I was hoping it would not rain until I got home from work.

After my workday ended, I was walking toward my car with a deep "whew," relieved not to be seeing any rain in sight. I started driving, concentrating on the road, and saw no sign of rain. I was in the parking area about three minutes from my house when little drops started falling onto my windshield. When I got inside the house, it started pouring down hard.

With deep appreciation, I immediately said, "Thank you, Jesus, for getting me home safely and holding back the rain." God's protection for His children is forever present in time of need. Hallelujah!

Psalm 46:1 (KJV): To the chief Musician for the sons of Korah, A Song upon Alamoth. God *is* our refuge and strength, a very present help in trouble.

76

Lovingly obliged word

Why am I easily offended? Why does this flesh seem to jail me through offenses? I had been seeking the Lord for answers, for release and peace. I was trusting the Lord to renew my mind and help relieve me of this flesh that wars against the Spirit of God. I believed I would be given peace through God's Word.

I was reading a book on love when it hit me. Jesus said, "Father, forgive them for they do not know what they are doing." This Word of revelation leaped right out at me. I jumped up with a big smile on my face, clapping my hands with joy because my answer had been given, and all I had to do was obey. I knew this answer came from heaven and that I had already been freed by the blood of Jesus. I needed guidance and understanding, and Jesus supplied it. Jesus is our loving Savior who lovingly applies His Word to those whose hearts long to please Him. His Word carries us to live out our lives in Him, for He is God alone, and there is no other.

Luke 23:34 (ESV): And Jesus said, "Father, forgive them, for they know not what they do." And they cast lots to divide his garments.

Matthew 6:33 (ESV): But seek first the kingdom of God and his righteousness, and all these things will be added to you.

77

Wowed by His thoughtfulness

How our hearts can bring us to a loving designation stamped by our Father's love. This year, I was yearning to bless some loved ones with gifts, but it did not look like I was going to have the money. Then something happened unexpectedly. I went in to work, and, surprisingly my manager said we could pick out anything we wanted up to fifty dollars. I stopped in my tracks with mouth wide open, eyebrows raised, thinking to myself, *is this really happening?*

She said, "We can pick out anything in our department, and believe me, we have a lot of great products in our department." Still in shock, I started picking out gifts for my loved ones. However, part of me wanted to buy for myself. But I kept thinking that the Lord had just blessed me to bless others, and I did not have to come up with the money to do it. I was not going to let this opportunity the Lord gave me be overtaken by selfishness.

As I was picking out the gifts, I continued to praise the Lord for everything I could think of. The more I praised Him, the more His presence wowed me. God gave me the desire of my heart, making it possible to bless others with gifts. Thank you, Jesus, for your lovingkindness. Hallelujah!

Numbers 23:20 (NASB): "Behold, I have received a command to bless; When He has blessed, then I cannot revoke it…"

78

God rewards private work

The Spirit of the Lord made something clear to me for my good. What a correction catcher it was for me. When my sales at work were good, I felt a need to tell one of the managers what I had done. Now, let me explain. I asked the Lord to increase the sales in my department, on my part, of course. I desired recognition from my leaders. My flesh was seeking to make itself known there. I was pushing myself very hard, but it did not seem right.

I had to stop what I was doing and deliberately right myself through Jesus. I tried to take authority over my fleshly desire, but then I remembered that my body belongs to the Lord. The Spirit of the Lord made it clear, "No one on my job was my reward. Only He is my reward."

It became very clear to me that I was to work unto God alone because He receives all the honor, glory, and praise. I realized I did not need to blow my own horn. God said He sees what we do in private and will reward us. Working unto the Lord privately is good enough for me, for He is the Creator of Heaven and Earth and everything in it. Jesus is sufficient. Hallelujah!

Matthew 6:6 (NLT): But when you pray, go away by yourself, shut the door behind you, and pray to your Father in private. Then your Father, who sees everything, will reward you.

79

Journeyed reflection

One Sunday afternoon as I entered a popular clothing store to buy an item for a loved one named Mackenzie, I felt like I was walking into a reflection from the past. Everything seemed so familiar but distant and disconnected.

While I was browsing around shopping for a blouse, I was observing people's faces and reactions toward what they were buying and how it would look on them. It reminded me of myself. I felt like I was going on a journey into the past.

This journey around the store spoke to me in silent pictures of how I used to be engaged with and focused on my outward appearance. I am not saying there is anything wrong with grooming ourselves to look nice. I am speaking of a person who is solely focused on self and their appearance.

I was always going shopping to beautify myself, to be looked at as a display in the eyes of people. My dressing to a T was always an attention getter, and I made sure of it. It gave me temporary relief to know that someone was noticing me. To be noticed meant, at times, I love you, you look great, you're smart, and so on.

As I kept roaming around in the store observing people, it was like looking out of a window into the past. My reflection showed me that my life has totally changed. It revealed that I had carried a false identity of myself and did not know it at that time.

In that reflection of my past, my energies were focused on how I could look better tomorrow than I did yesterday, and I made plans accordingly. The outside was the only thing that mattered to me at that time.

During this reflection, I continued to shop and observe. I saw such emptiness and longing for attention and love in the people, as I had felt once upon a time. I had substituted receiving love on the inside for dressing up for attention on the outside. I decorated myself on the outside and put myself up as a display, much like a mannequin in a storefront window. Oh, how it seemed I needed this attention for my self-worth.

As I was reflecting in the store, I saw so many people who craved desperately for attention through dressing up and exposing themselves as a dressed-up commodity. I was saddened by this because I spent years focusing on the outside and dressing to attract, thinking that was my answer to being loved and noticed.

I saw clearly through this reflection that it was a cry from the inside out. I knew because I had lived it and experienced a life filled with emptiness.

For a moment, I was able to feel the emptiness of the people around me and knew they were in desperate need of a Savior.

I have come to know that focusing on grooming the outside without knowing the love of Christ on the inside is like a downward spiral of something you're reaching for but will never receive if you do not know Jesus.

This dress-up display is admired for a short while, and then it fades until you buy another outfit to get more attention. I pretended to be happy because of the clothes I wore, and my emptiness seemed to be hidden well. Looking back, the people I hung around were the same way.

I finally found a blouse for Mackenzie, and as I got in line to pay, a smile appeared on my face. I thought about Jesus' great love for us. We will never need to replace His love with any material things.

When Jesus came into my life, the need to dress up to be loved or seen all dwindled away. Jesus gave Himself for me in all my shame and emptiness.

There is nothing wrong with dressing to the T, but make sure that the inside of you is dressed to the T as well and filled with the love of Jesus Who never fades way. This way, you will always be dressed up with the love of Jesus from the inside out.

Now, the best fashion show I have in my life is the righteousness of God through Christ Jesus. This assures me that I am always dressed to the T.

Guess what? This complete love of the Father flows from the inside out, and it never runs out. Jesus' love for me makes me beautiful, whole, and loved.

Hallelujah!

Ephesians 4:21-24 (NLT): Since you have heard about Jesus and have learned the truth that comes from him, throw off your old sinful nature and your former way of life, which is corrupted by lust and deception. Instead, let the Spirit renew your thoughts and attitudes. Put on your new nature, created to be like God—truly righteous and holy.

80

God's Word has your best interest

The Spirit of the Lord said to me, "I cannot hear you."

"Why do You say that?" I asked.

The Spirit of the Lord continued, "Observe who you are listening to all the time in gospel music and teaching tapes."

"Hmm." I started to think about how my time was being used, and I realized that I was hardly giving any personal time to the Holy Spirit to speak to me and guide me. Listening to preachers and gospel tapes are fine, but I should not have let those things dominate my time in place of Jesus.

A direct, personal word from the Spirit of the Lord has great meaning to me and always has a life changing effect, always brings good to me. After all, Jesus affirmed that His sheep know His voice. So, how am I going to keep being familiar with His voice if I am not listening to it all the time? Sometimes, listening to other teachings and music drowns out whatever the Spirit of God may be trying to say to get your attention.

Although God speaks through others, I love and treasure listening to my Father God who speaks personally to me. It is of the upmost value to listen to a loving Savior Who has your best interest for eternal life. God speaking to me is having something precious deposited into my heart that transforms, enlightens, protects, and most importantly, saves.

God spoke His words of life to great people like Isaiah, Moses, David, Paul, and so on. I am no different because I am His sheep, too, and I desire to hear His voice. No one could have done the things God did through those men who listened to Him.

I believe anything that is delivered via the voice of God is powerful. His ways are higher than our ways, and His thoughts are higher than our thoughts.

When we are listening to our Savior, there should not be anything to distract us from hearing and getting understanding. To listen and obey the voice of the Lord pleases Him. This shows we are followers of Christ Jesus.

Wow! What great instructions we have available to us with assurance. A willingness to experience God's abundant love through listening intently and purposefully with an obedient heart given to Him alone.

Hallelujah!

Isaiah 30:21 (NLT): Your own ears will hear him. Right behind you a voice will say, "This is the way you should go," whether to the right or to the left.

Proverbs 2:2 (NASB): ... Make your ear attentive to wisdom, Incline your heart to understanding ...

81

Magnificence revealed from God's spoken word

The Holy Spirit explained and made clear to me the importance of His Word, and He instructed me not to allow others to convince me otherwise. It is understood that the Word was from the beginning, and it was the Word that brought life to the face of the earth.

The Holy Spirit gave me examples in my life of how the Word has brought manifestations, such as my present work, breath brought back into my mom's body, health restored in my husband's body, provided finances so we would have a place to live, money received miraculously to provide for our needs, my husband being hired on the spot with a great job, and the list goes on and on. I believe God's Word manifested all things that were provided for us.

I was reminded that the Word of God is life. When it is spoken with a believing heart, life is revealed, along with the glory of the Lord and His magnificence and eternal grace.

Sometimes, I remain still and observe the sky, ocean, trees, mountains, plants, animals, and other nature-related things. I do this because it allows me to keep things in perspective. God spoke all of these things into existence by faith. They did not exist until God spoke them into existence with His Word.

God's Word is filled with power, manifesting the very things He speaks. His Word is presently provided for us to use for encouragement, correction, wisdom, understanding, comfort, protection, and our whole life on this earth.

God's children can enjoy the most powerful faith through the Holy Spirit Who was given to us so that we and others will always be able to see the salvation of the Lord through His wonderful works.

Hallelujah!

Acts 14:3 (ESV): So they remained for a long time, speaking boldly for the Lord, who bore witness to the word of his grace, granting signs and wonders to be done by their hands.

John 1:1 (NASB): In the beginning was the Word, and the Word was with God, and the Word was God.

82

Healing was done for me, too

hy do you speak the Word over someone else's life and not your own? The Spirit of the Lord spoke to me clearly. I had spoken God's Word over my Aunt Anita, who was in the hospital at the time, saying, "By the stripes of Jesus Christ, she is healed."

I believed and was convinced that Jesus provided healing for us over two thousand years ago through His death, burial, and resurrection. But I knew there must have been something I needed to learn for the Spirit of the Lord to have addressed this question to me.

Then, something happened. A test showed up, to see if I believed what I was saying over Aunt Anita.

My right nostril was very sore to touch and had a knot inside of it. It had lasted for three or four days. I was going about my business and continuing to do the things I needed to do, but the soreness was annoying and painful. The Spirit of the Lord stopped me in my tracks and said, "Why are you speaking My Word over someone else but not over yourself? Do you not believe it for yourself?"

I pondered His questions and realized there must have been some unconscious doubt regarding my own healing. I had to examine my heart and ask myself if I believed the truth that Jesus had taken our infirmities and removed our diseases.

As I continued to ponder His questions, I knew for sure that God is no respecter of persons. Therefore, I knew that Jesus loves me as well as everyone else. His Spirit of Truth is deposited in me confirming what He has already done for me, and this includes healing.

One thing I realized in examining myself with the questions that were presented by the Holy Spirit was that in times past, when I was ill, I seemed to ignore my symptoms and not speak the Word of Truth over my own life. At that point, I knew I had to build myself up in my most Holy faith regarding all that Jesus had done for me on the cross. He had already taken all of my sicknesses and diseases, as well as those of others, through His resurrection.

Then, all of the memories of Jesus' goodness began to come into my mind. He healed me through His Word, and I was able to witness all the signs and wonders Jesus had blessed me with come to pass.

With boldness I proclaimed, "By the stripes of Jesus Christ, I was healed!" My nostril was healed, and two days later, the knot was gone. Praise the Lord for the truth of His Word.

Hallelujah!

Matthew 8:17 (NLT): This fulfilled the word of the Lord through the prophet Isaiah, who said, "He took our sicknesses and removed our diseases."

Acts 10:34 (NLT): Then Peter replied, "I see very clearly that God shows no favoritism.

83

I clearly see His sent Word

Spending time with my grandmother, Rebecca, is always a pleasure. She is eighty-nine years old at the time of this writing. She has a sharp mind, does things on her own, loves to talk, laugh, and have fun.

As I was visiting with her at her place and enjoying our conversation, she asked me if I could put a vacuum cleaner together that she had ordered. I said yes, of course.

I opened the box, pulled out the directions, and started reading. As I was reading the directions, the Spirit of the Lord was speaking to me. My grandmother had no idea what was going on because I kept reading the directions.

Then I began putting the vacuum cleaner together. It was such a pleasure to receive an inspired Word from the Spirit of the Lord to help me understand what He wanted to show me.

The Spirit of the Lord said, "When you are reading these directions on how to put this item together, the person who made the item and created directions is not physically here with you. You are following his directions, putting all the parts together, and believing it will turn out the way it is supposed to. Now you see a finished product from directions sent to you to follow, and the person who wrote them was not even here physically."

The Spirit of the Lord continued on as I finished putting the vacuum cleaner together. He said, "This is exactly how I want you to trust and believe My Word. You cannot see Me, but My Spirit and My Word are there in your heart. This accomplishes My Will, and like you were able to see the finished product of the vacuum cleaner, so will you see the finished truths of My Word."

Sure enough, when I look at the sky, the trees, the ocean, and all the things He has provided for me, I clearly see the finished truths of His sent Word. Hallelujah!

Isaiah 55:11 (NLT): It is the same with my word. I send it out, and it always produces fruit. It will accomplish all I want it to, and it will prosper everywhere I send it.

84

The Spirit of Truth gives what I need to move forward

Jesus Christ always gives us His peace in all circumstances. When I realize I have done something that opposes God's Word, and I cannot shake it off, I seek my Father's guidance. Many times, when I'm seeking His wisdom, I seek with expectation and excitement. I know Jesus always has a loving truth for me, whether it is correction, encouragement, or both. Either way, both are encouraging to me.

Jesus always assures me of His presence to help me. Sometimes, I try to justify my wrong, but the more I try to work it out myself, the more my sin tries to barricade my thoughts, sending me into a state of discomfort.

When I go to my Lord with sincerity, pouring out and admitting all my wrong, an assurance of forgiveness comes forth. He overwhelms me with His peace, not holding anything against me.

Jesus gives me a way of escape, keeping me close to Him where I am able to hear His voice in time of need in the most loving way. The Spirit of Truth is always waiting for me to reach out and get what I need to move forward.

Matthew 11:28 (NLT): Then Jesus said, "Come to me, all of you who are weary and carry heavy burdens, and I will give you rest …"

85

Jesus' will is above distractions

Why do I feel so distracted when I first wake up in the morning? Why are my thoughts driving me to things that are not important? Gathering my thoughts and trying to prioritize them for daily success is not always easy.

These distractions take me to places and cause me to do things that are, at times, fruitless. What can I get out of these fruitless distractions? Nothing!

Getting up every morning and facing all of the things we have before us can be quite mind boggling. Many times, we are not aware that we have devoted ourselves to our distractions and not to a forward movement that leads to a fruitful life. The distractions have no eternal destiny with Jesus.

Can you imagine where this roadmap would lead us when we are distracted and off course? When waking up in the morning, I realize I have two choices to make—whether I want my thoughts to be on Jesus, or things that distract me from the peace that Jesus gives.

One of the best solutions to a distracted mind is to keep the mind stayed on Jesus. Setting the mind on things above is the answer to eliminating distractions. Setting my mind on Jesus, which is above distractions, brings me into a perfect peace that allows me to go about my day perfectly to His designation.

So, now I know that distractions rob us from the perfect will of God

Who knows His perfect will for us each and every day. By setting our minds on things above, we get our answers on how to start our days. And no matter whether I am being instructed, encouraged, or corrected, I can take hold of it and go forward without any feelings of distraction, while experiencing the peace that allows me to accomplish what is for my good, which is His will.

---

1 Corinthians 7:35 (NLT): I am saying this for your benefit, not to place restrictions on you. I want you to do whatever will help you serve the Lord best, with as few distractions as possible.

86
A hardened heart does not stop God's purpose

From past experiences, I learned that when you are in line with the purposes of God, no man can overthrow them, although it may appear like man is getting the upper hand, as it did with Pharaoh. But remember, God hardened Pharaoh's heart. Pharaoh thought he had power over our Father God, but he was in for a real awakening.

I remember when I lived in Virginia, I was working with a particular company for almost six years. I faithfully went to work before the time I was scheduled. I worked diligently and received great reviews. However, a situation happened that left me in fear of losing my job.

At the time, I was a single parent who needed work to take care of my son. My son had gotten sick, and I had to pick him up from school. I had to keep him out of school for almost two weeks. As he was feeling better, I suddenly got sick, and this caused me to be out of work for almost three weeks. Out of the years I had worked for this company, nothing like this had ever happened. I felt sure my manager, Jeff, would understand.

I returned to work to find an envelope lying on my chair. I opened the envelope, and I could not believe what I was reading. It must have been about four or five pages long. By the time I got to the second page, tears were rolling down my face. Suddenly, overwhelming, hurtful, angry, feelings started to take hold of me. I was threatened by Jeff's words.

Needless to say, my job was in jeopardy. Jeff was upset because we had proposals due for delivery. My position was very intense and critically important for the company. I was counted on to type and edit proposals and documents for special use.

At this point, I was being treated unfairly for being with my son when he was sick, and I was recovering from being sick as well. Jeff was much older than me and always displayed a "you're beneath me" attitude. I overlooked it as long as we both respected each other.

I was in my early twenties and was clueless about what I should do. I decided to let someone named Leo from another department, a man of great intelligence and someone I respected, review what Jeff documented to be put in my files. What Jeff had written would affect my raises if it went into my file. After Leo read the information, he politely put the paper down on his desk and responded, "I can't believe Jeff wrote something like this to you after all of the late nights you've stay at this place to get proposals done for him. This is what I'm going to do, Angela, because Jeff is taking advantage of you. Let me take this home, and I'm going to respond to each sentence line by line."

Jeff needed to deal with someone on Leo's level. Leo took the papers home and responded line by line. After Leo finished, he brought the papers back to me to look over. If I had any changes, we would change them together.

Leo and I collaborated together, making sure everything was responded to line by line. He instructed me to do the same thing Jeff did to me. Jeff just happened to be on a short vacation, so Leo advised me to put it on his chair. It would be the first thing he saw when he walked into his office.

I was so excited about Jeff returning to work, but I did not know what to expect. Either way it was done, and I would have to await the outcome. Jeff arrived and went into his office. He closed the door, and it was very quiet. I felt as though I was watching a suspense movie and did not know what the next move would be. About fifteen minutes passed. I was sure Jeff was as shocked as I had been when he read what was in the envelope.

Jeff finally came out and asked me to come into his office. I politely walked in and sat down. He asked me what my response was all about. My nerves must have taken over. I expressed to Jeff all the nights I had stayed up doing proposals and documents to have ready for presentations and delivery. I told him that my son had to stay with the babysitter overnight many nights because I was there working for him, making sure everything was done. By this time, my tears were flowing.

Jeff knew I was hurt and was telling the truth. I had sacrificed many nights with my son because I was there working. I really let him have it. I told him that I felt taken advantaged of and that he did not even think about my needing to be with my son while he was sick, nor me for that matter. After I let it all out, I stated that if he put what he had written in my file, I would put what I wrote as a defense.

Then I could not believe the sweet words that came out of Jeff's mouth. He responded that we would just put this behind us. I said okay but that I would be checking my file periodically. I then got up and walked back to my desk.

I told Leo everything that happened. He was extremely happy for me. I expressed to Leo how grateful I was for his help in my time of need. I know it was the Lord Jesus Christ who used Leo to accomplish His purpose for my good.

Jeff, like Pharaoh, thought he would defeat me. He wanted to keep me under his oppressive tactics. Jeff could not overthrow God's purpose for me in this situation. It turned out that Jeff's plans were cast down and defeated, just like Pharaoh's plans crashed in the sea.

Hallelujah!

---

2 Chronicles 25:8 **(KJV):** But if thou wilt go, do it, be strong for the battle: God shall make thee fall before the enemy: for God hath power to help, and to cast down.

87

Living in Jesus' perfect truth

I have always felt drawn to Acts 17:28, but I did not know why I felt my life was connected to it. But to know that I live, move, and have my being in Christ Jesus gave me great comfort.

I knew this verse related a true description of me being in a place of honor and love. This Spirit of Truth grasps me as if I am cradled in Christ Jesus' arms, wanting to know more of how I live, move, and have my being in Him.

I decided to research the meaning of this Scripture to get better understanding, when the Spirit of the Lord said, "Stop, I will explain it to you! Just listen!"

When the Holy Spirit spoke to me, I got down on my knees there in our guest bedroom, which is my quiet place. I was very still as I listened anxiously and attentively.

The Spirit of the Lord said, "You know how you live in your house. You do many things there, such as wash dishes, wash clothes, clean house, read. You accomplish all of your chores in this one place. Your very being is moving to get things done.

"Likewise, in Me, I AM is where you live. I AM your home, and you move to do what pleases Me, you move to do things that glorify Me. Living in Me is that perfect place where miraculous things happens, such as laying hands on the sick, proclaiming the Good News, setting the captives free, encouraging and loving others, forgiving others, praying for others, and so much more."

I am grateful for Jesus personally explaining and giving me understanding of the truth of His Word. We are indeed His offspring.

Understanding this Scripture, that in Him we live, and move, and have our being, has certainly given me confidence and assurance that I can accomplish His plan for the life He has given me.

Hallelujah!

Acts 17:28 (ESV): ... for "In him we live and move and have our being'; as even some of your own poets have said, For we are indeed his offspring."

88

Hallelujah time in the parking lot

On my way to work, I stopped by the grocery store to pick up an item. As I was leaving the store and approaching my car, a lady was getting out of her car very slowly. She said sweetly, "Your hair is beautiful."

I thanked her, and in return, I complimented her hair because I love the color and style of her hair. She responded, "Thank you."

When she got out of the car, I noticed she was limping, so I said, "I noticed you are limping. Are you okay?" She responded, "I just got off work, and my ankles are hurting." I asked her if I could pray for her.

She answered yes, and then she hesitated for a second and said, "I need to know in whose name." I said, "In Jesus' Name." She responded excitedly, "Yes, yes, please do!" I told her that Jesus' name is above every name. She agreed with me joyfully.

I knelt there in the parking lot and laid my hands on both of her ankles, commanding every ligament and bone in her ankles to straighten out in the Name of Jesus! I commanded her ankles to be made whole in the Name of Jesus!

While I was praying for her, she asked me to also pray for her knees. I commanded her knees to straighten up and recover in the Name of Jesus!

She started bending her knees, moving her ankles, and shouting with joy that they felt better. She embraced me with tears, saying thank you. I answered, "To God be the Glory. Let us thank Him." She said, "That's right!"

In her embrace, she blessed me with wonderful words of encouragement. We parted with the joy of the Lord pouring out His love as always and showing His faithfulness!

Hallelujah!

---

1 Peter 3:8 (KJV): Finally, be ye all of one mind, having compassion one of another, love as brethren, be pitiful, be courteous …

89

Truth drove anxiousness out

Anxiousness had overtaken me. How had I allowed this to happen to me on my job? I knew the Lord Jesus had opened this door for me for His Glory, so why was I so afraid of not doing a good job and possibly losing it at any time?

Why had I given my work so much power over me that I was living underneath a cover of fear?

Why did it seem like I was so engrossed in seeking to please those who had charge over me at my work place?

I began to seek the Lord's guidance in the midst of my mental discomfort. I wanted relief from the anxious thoughts of pleasing men. I had allowed this torment to imprison my mind, causing great uneasiness.

I absolutely love the work the Lord had given me to do unto Him, but how could I grab hold of His peace while working there?

I started seeking the Lord Jesus for His help. I wanted to do exactly what Jesus said, to seek Him first, because I knew the answers were in Him, and I would not have to look any further.

I thought about the many times I had sought out answers from others first with the result that they had no words of peace or comfort for me.

No more! Not this time! The Lord Jesus brought me my answer. He brought me peace that relieved my troubled mind. He gave me Colossians

3:23-24 that says, "Whatever you do, work heartily, as for the Lord and not for men ... You are serving the Lord Christ" (ESV).

When I meditated on this Scripture that the Holy Spirit had given to me, all of my fears made an exit and confidence made an entrance, causing the peace of God to be exalted in my heart.

Thank you, Jesus, for Your Spirit of Truth that is always available, giving me confidence in time of need!

Hallelujah!

Hebrews 4:16 (ESV): Let us then with confidence draw near to the throne of grace, that we may receive mercy and find grace to help in time of need.

90

A prayer blessed someone in the breakroom

While I was on my break at work, before I started to eat, I bowed my head and blessed the food. When I finished praying, a gentleman on the right side of the table gazed at me for a couple of seconds and then said, "That was beautiful."

I questioned, "What?"

He said, "I've never seen anything like that before."

Again, I repeated, "What?"

The gentleman responded, "I have never seen anyone pray here."

As I was listening to him there in the breakroom, there were others at the table as well. I was surprised by his expression of amazement at me blessing my food.

I did not know how to respond to him at that moment, but there was a joy that welled up on the inside of me, thinking that he saw Jesus in me, and it made him very happy.

For a moment, I thought about what he had said, that he had never seen anyone pray in the breakroom. He had never witnessed workers praying over their food. I thought about how people miss out on the blessing of giving thanks and blessing for the food God provides.

The most extraordinary blessing in this situation was that I was recognized as a witness for Christ in the breakroom for giving an appreciation

prayer to my Father Who provides food for us.
　　Hallelujah!

Matthew 5:16 (NLT): In the same way, let your good deeds shine out for all to see, so that everyone will praise your heavenly Father.

91

Trials build godly character

Sometimes, when I am going about my day, I suddenly find myself in the midst of a trial without understanding why it is happening. At first, it seems distressing and discouraging. Then, I think about God's Word, and it presents an opportunity to be strengthened as I build and gain the character of God. Most of all, He is glorified, and the fruit of my lips can continue to give Him thanks in the middle of the trial.

At times, we seem to be going through a dark tunnel that is forever long with no one around to rescue us. But, praise the Lord, He is always present in times of need and able to deliver us from every trial.

The Holy Spirit gave me His Word that caused me to align my thoughts with His thoughts and put them in His perfect peace. Looking at trials as opportunities to see God's glory and to gain maturity in Christ is an ongoing journey toward experiencing God's great joy and love.

James 1:2 (NLT): Dear brothers and sisters, when troubles of any kind come your way, consider it an opportunity for great joy.

92

Patience opens doors

How sweet it is to love others who have not yet found Jesus and to be patient with them. I reflect back to a time when I thought I had always believed because I was raised in church. How deceived I was for years not knowing I was in a dark place separated from God.

I remember so well when Jesus called and found me. The great Rescuer saved me that day. The darkness of my life was illuminated by the blood of my Savior. I will forever be grateful to Jesus for snatching me out of the fire.

I appreciate all of His patience with me before and after that day. His patience has helped me to understand that, by Jesus' example, I must be patient with others as He is with me. This love and patience with others exemplifies the very essence of Jesus taking our place on the cross.

As we choose the way of being patient with others through the love of Christ, it allows them to see Jesus in a way that prepares them for receiving Him as their Lord and Savior. They will be able to reflect and say that they saw the love of God in him or her.

I remember a time when I was in darkness, that same place where someone else may be. There were loving believers in Christ Jesus who were patient with me, and I recalled their commitment to Christ in loving me when I was unlovable.

Thank you, Jesus, for your loving Body who showed forth Your Spirit in loving me. This is the aroma of God through Christ everywhere we go, exemplifying Christ knocking at the door, waiting for it to be opened.

Ephesians 2:12-13 (NIV): ... remember that at that time you were separate from Christ, excluded from citizenship in Israel and foreigners to the covenants of the promise, without hope and without God in the world. But now in Christ Jesus you who once were far away have been brought near by the blood of Christ.

Revelation 3:20 (NIV): Here I am! I stand at the door and knock. If anyone hears my voice and opens the door, I will come in and eat with that person, and they with me.

93

Stop at the counsel of God

After seeking the Lord Jesus for the solution to a problem and receiving His answer, which gave me total peace, I then sought an answer from someone else.

The Spirit of the Lord stopped me in my tracks and said, "Why are you still seeking the thoughts of the flesh?" When I receive an answer from Him, it stops there. There is no reason to seek an answer elsewhere.

The lesson I learned was to trust Jesus and all of His perfect answers to my situations, circumstances, and problems. The God Who created heaven and earth and everything in it knows everything, and He certainly knows the answer to any problem we have.

God's Word says that He works everything out for our good. I really do believe that because whenever I do things His way, not only does it come out for my good, but it comes out for the good of all those around me.

Reflecting back on Shadrach, Meshach, and Abednego, we see that their full trust was in the Lord God. They did not seek any advice from anyone, nor did they seek their own fleshly advice. Their minds were settled in trusting the Lord, and they would serve no other gods nor worship the golden image.

Our Heavenly Father is all-knowing and the best Counselor. Therefore, we need not seek counsel from any other when the answer has been given to us by the Holy Spirit.

The lesson I learned was not to seek the counsel of man, when God has given His Spirit of Truth.

---

1 Kings 22:5 (NIV): But Jehoshaphat also said to the king of Israel, "First seek the counsel of the LORD."

1 John 2:27 (HCSB): The anointing you received from Him remains in you, and you don't need anyone to teach you. Instead, His anointing teaches you about all things and is true and is not a lie; just as He has taught you, remain in Him.

94

Jesus' presence dispatches His plans

I have contemplated so many times on how to please Jesus, how to deepen my desire to do His will. I started to reflect on my life and noticed that the more I meditated on His Word, the more I wanted to be in His Word. The more I saw His glory, the more I desired to see His glory.

I always want to be with Him, to hear His truth, feel His comfort, and even receive His corrections. Whatever plans God has for me, I want my desire to be obeying them.

Abiding in Jesus and Him abiding in me dispatches all of the plans He has for me. He is guiding my steps in the ways that please Him. How awesome is that? Very awesome!

Hallelujah!

Jeremiah 29:11 (NLT): "... For I know the plans I have for you," says the LORD. "They are plans for good and not for disaster, to give you a future and a hope ..."

95

Heart change through a loss

How was it that the loss was so painful? It was just a material thing. It was our first beautiful home, and we felt so blessed. The home had large picture windows that reflected sunlight in every part of the house. Every room had a special meaning because of our grandchildren, our family, and friends who left precious memories. The home gave me the opportunity to serve with love as we welcomed our family and friends. They left with great memories of our shared fellowship, eager for the next time. I found out quickly that sometimes there is no next time in the things we enjoy.

I used to think about God's Word that speaks of things fading away, never taking into consideration that it included the things I felt He had given me. Oh, how God's truth can illuminate our lives. He will purge everything that may try to separate us from His love. When I reflect on my relationship with my Father God while living in that house, it was not as close as it is now.

I felt embarrassed at losing our first home. Pain and anger analyzed it as a personal failure, as though I did not deserve it, and that is why we lost it. We moved from our four-bedroom, three-bath home to a small two-bedroom, one-bath apartment.

For a while, I refrained from having company. I was overwhelmed with shame. I noticed there were times when I felt relieved at being in a smaller place and not having the many responsibilities of caring for a large home. At other times, I felt myself torn between where I used to live and where I was living then.

Then I went to God's Word to get understanding of what had happened. In seeking Him through His Word, I first realized that when I was in the other house, He was not first in my life. I had to be honest with God and myself regarding where my heart was when I was living in that house. He did not have my all in all.

Living in the apartment and seeking Him first made me understand clearly that no matter where I am, I must seek Jesus first. Now I understand that it is because when things do fade away, or you lose them, they will not affect you if you did not put the things of the world first. When you seek the Kingdom of God first and not the things of the world, your heart will not be troubled from losing material things.

Being in the presence of the peace of God, seeking Him first, I have experienced being shielded from the effects of the world. Now I understand the pain that Jesus wanted to shield me from. Losing our home showed me where my heart had been and where it needed to be with Christ Jesus. My relationship with Christ Jesus has changed my heart, reflecting great understanding of His love.

Now I know the importance of seeking first the Kingdom of God and His righteousness. It affirms to my heart that I am always accepted in the Beloved, no matter what sudden changes come my way.

Psalm 34:18 (NLT): The LORD is close to the brokenhearted; he rescues those whose spirits are crushed.

96

Reminds me that He abides

My manager did not know where the product belonged. I was surprised because I thought he would have known where all the products belonged, since he had worked in that department for so long.

I had about eight minutes left on the clock before my shift ended, and he pulled a particular product out of the box and said, "I never know where this product goes."

I looked at the product, and honestly, I did not know where it belonged either. Although I was still new in that department, I whispered under my breath and said, "Lord, will You please tell me where the product belongs before I leave?"

I said to my manager, "I usually read the back of the product, and sometimes it will give me a clue of where to place it."

He said, "So do I." He looked on the back of the product and read out loud what was printed there.

I asked, "Did you look in *this* section?"

He answered, "Yes, I looked several times."

Then, immediately, the Holy Spirit directed me to the exact location of where similar products were located. I lifted my finger and said excitedly to my manager, "Here it is!"

He hurried over to where I was and said, "You're brilliant."

He departed quickly, and I stood there, bowed my head, and whispered, "Thank you, Jesus. To God be the glory."

I love the way the Holy Spirit helped me right at the moment when I needed Him. He often reminds me that He abides in me and I in Him.

Hallelujah!!

John 15:7 (ESV): If you abide in me, and my words abide in you, ask whatever you wish, and it will be done for you.

97

Boldness in me

The Spirit of the Lord said, "You do not have to ask for boldness. My Spirit Who lives in you is bold. You do not have to ask for joy. My Spirit in you is full of joy. When I go with your mouth and tell you what to say, it will be like fire coming out of your mouth. Never fear what I instruct you to say. My Spirit always knows what to say to pierce the hearts of the people. My Spirit is complete in you and cannot be shaken. Be strong in My Spirit Who is in you. Time is drawing near for you to speak My Word with power and grace."

Matthew 10:20 (NLT): For it is not you who will be speaking—it will be the Spirit of your Father speaking through you.

98

Living through Christ's mindset

A miraculous transformation took place in my life recently after listening to a minister teaching on being seated with Christ and the benefits of being seated on the right hand of the Father in Christ Jesus.

In the past, I did not have an understanding of this truth. Gaining understanding of being seated with Christ has renewed my mind and released me from insecurities that were keeping me in bondage. I gained a renewed confidence in Him. Now I know I can do all things through Christ. All things are possible according to His will.

Being assured of my position with Christ Jesus has also given me the assurance that I am always filled with His love, knowledge, and guidance.

Being seated with Christ has changed how I walk out my life. Prior to this, I thought about myself more than others. Now that my life has reversed, all I think about is how and what I can do for other people to bring joy to them through Jesus. I talk to my constant Friend about ways I can be a light in all situations. He always has an answer for me.

One example was when someone was deliberately being unkind to me. His truth reminded me to think about how He was so very kind to us when He took all of our sins and said, "Father, forgive them for they know not what they do." Jesus affirmed that if we would look at situations like this and remember that He has already overcome the world for us, we would be acceptable in His sight, and others would see His light shining through us.

He taught that instead of being offended by the way someone speaks or the way they treat me, I should look at them as being in need of a Savior. This changed my mindset and gave me an understanding of being seated with Christ Jesus.

Another benefitting truth of my being seated with Christ is that I am more than a conqueror in Him. Being seated with Him has brought to me, straight from heaven, instructions to implement. When I follow these instructions, the result is something I could never have done on my own.

The reality of being seated with Christ Jesus gives me the confidence to boldly accomplish His will. Being seated with Christ Jesus has rescued me from a low self-esteem to an inspired position in Him.

Hallelujah!

Ephesians 2:6 (ESV): ... and raised us up with him and seated us with him in the heavenly places in Christ Jesus ...

2 Corinthians 5:17 (NLT): This means that anyone who belongs to Christ has become a new person. The old life is gone; a new life has begun!

99

You are waiting on Me and no one else

I was thinking about the finished draft of this book and submitting my manuscript to a publisher. I wondered how long the process would take before I would receive a response.

Then the Spirit of the Lord said so informatively, "Thank Me when you receive a no and thank Me when you receive the yes!"

I began to read the Word and a Scripture jumped out at me: "Wait on the Lord, be of good courage, and He shall strengthen thine heart: wait I say, on the Lord."

I pondered this Scripture for a while, and then the Spirit of the Lord said, "You are waiting on Me, not your editor, publisher, yourself, or anyone else." He continued, "If anyone says no regarding your book, stand still and see the salvation of the Lord like you have seen in times past. I AM still the same today as I was yesterday!" Hallelujah!

Psalm 27:14 (NLT): Wait patiently for the LORD. Be brave and courageous. Yes, wait patiently for the LORD.

Isaiah 40:31 (ESV): … but they who wait for the LORD shall renew their strength; they shall mount up with wings like eagles; they shall run and not be weary; they shall walk and not faint.

100

Personal prescription given by the Holy Spirit

Symptoms of a cold were trying to invade my body. I was scheduled to work on Tuesday and was considering not going, but I needed to be there to attend a class. I decided to attend the class and leave afterward because my nose was dripping continuously.

After class, I was scheduled to go out on the floor to help customers, but I did not feel it was appropriate to be in customers' faces while I was sneezing and dripping mucus.

During our class, they gave us a 30-minute break. I called my husband to pick me up after my class. But let me back up a little.

Before my class started, I went to one of my co-workers, Velda, expressing my discomfort at working under those conditions. Velda understood because she could hear and see that I was congested. She gave me something for the cold and gave me instructions on how to take it to insure that I would feel better. She also instructed me to take it before going to class. I did not take it right then because I wanted to wait and start it when I got home.

When I arrived home, I was about to take the cold syrup when the Spirit of the Lord said, "Do not take it." He said, "I want you to praise Me all day because this is a circumstance." That caused me to remember that months before, the Holy Spirit had led me to a Scripture saying to praise

God in all circumstances.

The Holy Spirit brought that Scripture back to my memory. I was given my own personal prescription from the Holy Spirit. I was to focus on praising Him all day Monday and Tuesday, take my vitamin C and drink the lemon juice. Then I would feel better and be ready to work on Wednesday. I obeyed His voice and saw the manifestation of His healing power revealed.

Listening and obeying the Holy Spirit led me to an awesome experience in Jesus. After all, Jesus gave a miraculous prescription to the blind man. He took him by the hand and led him out of the village, and when he had spat on his eyes and laid his hands on him, he asked him, "Do you see anything?" The man looked up and said, "I see people, but they look like trees, walking." Then Jesus laid his hands on his eyes again. When he opened his eyes, his sight was restored, and he saw everything clearly. Thank you, Lord Jesus, for the healing prescription.

Hallelujah!

Mark 8:23 (KJV): And he took the blind man by the hand, and led him out of the town; and when he had spit on his eyes, and put his hands upon him, he asked him if he saw ought.

Psalm 103:20 (ESV): Bless the LORD, O you his angels, you mighty ones who do his word, obeying the voice of his word!

101

Healing during closing hours

My Father, through His Son, Jesus Christ, gave me the most wonderful experience. A co-worker named Brian had been sick with a cold for about three weeks, and it seemed like he could not shake it off. When Brian finally returned to work, we were scheduled to close the store that evening, but he was not feeling well at all.

Brian and I started doing our closing duties for the store, although it was not yet the closing hour. As we were working, Brian kept expressing how bad he felt and that none of the medications he was taking seemed to work. I was able to tell he was not feeling well because he was not his usual vibrant self, bouncing around the store.

As we were working, I was listening to Brian carefully, and in my heart I wanted to say and do something that was risky while working in the store. So I hesitated because of where we were, and I did not know if it was the right time.

As Brian continued to express his uncomfortable situation, out came my question, "Do you believe in healing?" He said, "I believe in anything." Then I asked, "Do you believe in healing in the name of Jesus?" He said, "Yes," with boldness!

At the time I was speaking to Brian I was up on my stepladder. I stepped down and asked him if I could pray for him, and surprisingly, he said, "Yes." I asked Brian if I could lay hands on him. He said, "Yes."

I began to command every sickness and disease to leave his body and for his body to be made whole in the name of Jesus! I explained to Brian that Jesus took all of our sicknesses and diseases when He died for us over two thousand years ago.

I believe Jesus' healing power overtook him because his whole demeanor changed. The Lord made it possible for His light to shine through His love expressed in the work place. The Lord has awesome timing because I noticed, at the time, no customers were in the department. I believe Jesus did it that way so He would be glorified and remembered by Brian. What a wonderful Savior we abide in and Who abides in us to do His will in the timing He chooses.

Mark 1:41 (NASB): Moved with compassion, Jesus stretched out His hand and touched him, and said to him, "I am willing; be cleansed."

102

Cancer has no residence in the Kingdom

What a marvelous day it was. A man came into our whole-body department asking for suggestions for high blood pressure. I directed him to the section where we shelve the blood pressure selections.

As we stood there viewing the products, he turned and gazed at me as if he knew Christ lived in me. He started sharing his challenges and what the doctor had said. He was struggling with the report.

We introduced ourselves, and I gave Johnny my full attention. Again, like before, there were no customers or managers around to distract Johnny from sharing his concerns about his health report from the doctor. But what came out of Johnny's mouth next was, "I don't agree with those doctors."

I emphatically agreed with Johnny's decision to disagree with the doctor's report. Then the Holy Spirit activated in me. Before I knew it, I boldly commanded the cancer to leave Johnny's body. I rebuked satan, reminding him that Johnny's body belonged to the Lord Jesus Christ.

Johnny was so overwhelmed with the joy of the Lord, he said in a loud voice, "I'm about to run through this store!"

At this point, I realized I had to get hold of myself because I was at work. I was silently thinking, *I hope Johnny doesn't run through this store.*

But if Johnny did, I was not going to stop him from praising the Lord.

Johnny started to shed tears, saying that he knew he was supposed to meet me. We both thanked Jesus for his healing, and then Johnny departed, or at least I thought he did.

Ten or fifteen minutes later, Johnny was back, still thanking the Lord Jesus for his healing. We both started thanking Jesus again for this assured blessing. And as Johnny was walking off, he gazed at me again as he had done when we first met.

Johnny thanked me for agreeing with him for his healing that had already taken place in eternity. Cancer has no residence in the Kingdom of God.

Hallelujah!

Mark 1:41 (NASB): Moved with compassion, Jesus stretched out His hand and touched him, and said to him, "I am willing; be cleansed."

103

Aroma of love to the unkind

It is such an honor to express true love to others who are acting unloving and to be kind to those who are unkind. The Spirit of the Lord was encouraging me about how wonderful it is to be presented with opportunities like these.

Believe me, it seems like these opportunities come more frequently than I would like, but as I pass the test in my endeavors to be loving when encountering these situations, my character seems to look more and more like Christ. This is what I desire.

At times, I do miss the mark. It is exciting, however, to be given another opportunity to pass the test with the help of the Holy Spirit. And as I pass the test, God's character is being formed in me.

As I am put in a position to be kind and loving to someone who presents a difficult and unattractive behavior, it is an opportunity to reveal Jesus' love to them.

Someone who behaves in an unkind way may be trapped in thoughts that no one loves them or cares. This is where we come in with the love of Jesus to show them what love looks like and how it is expressed. We are able to help them without them even asking for help.

We are to respect and obey those who have authority over us and not be affected by their unattractive behavior. It is God Whom we are trying to please.

When Jesus' love is shown to an unkind heart, it is like a light that shines brightly in the darkness. Jesus' presence shows love in a way that an unkind person has probably never experienced before.

Jesus uses the members of His body to give out a sweet aroma of love that is not affected or offended by an unkind heart. This was clearly shown at the Cross when we sinned against Him, and He loved us anyway. What a wonderful example of His gracious love for us.

Christ Jesus sees us through His love, and we are to see others through the love of Christ. As we mature in Christ, we are conformed to His image, so that others see only Christ's reflection of love and kindness in us. Then they, too, will experience the aroma of love from Jesus Christ.

Luke 6:35-36 (NLT): "Love your enemies! Do well to them. Lend to them without expecting to be repaid. Then your reward from heaven will be very great, and you will truly be acting as children of the Most High, for he is kind to those who are unthankful and wicked. You must be compassionate, just as your Father is compassionate ..."

104

In Him is treasure

My experience of being accepted in the Beloved is being shielded with eternal salvation, love, peace, joy, protection, and so much more. All of this comes with being in Jesus.

I arose that day and said to the Holy Spirit, "Holy Spirit, I want to do everything in You today. I desire to love others, to be a dedicated and honest worker, to be kind and loving to others, all in You.

As I continued communicating with the Holy Spirit, I reminded Him, "I can't do it without You, Holy Spirit."

I asked Him with sincerity, "Holy Spirit, show Yourself in me so everyone will see You and draw near to You. I will live, move, and have my being in You alone.

In this place in You, I am comforted, loved, born-again, rescued, and protected. Being in You, Holy Spirit, I follow You with assurance knowing that with every step, You are with me and are teaching me the way I should go.

Hebrews 13:21 (NLT): … may he equip you with all you need for doing his will. May He produce in you, through the power of Jesus Christ, every good thing that is pleasing to Him. All glory to Him forever and ever! Amen.

105

Your insecurities have no power

A beautiful day had begun with my husband blessing me by taking me out for lunch. As we arrived home, I had a couple of hours before going to work, so I decided to spend quiet time with the Holy Spirit, which is always a wonderful experience.

I entered my prayer room where the Spirit of the Lord and I have intimate conversations with one another, with tremendous and meaningful wisdom given to me that inspires my days. This intimate gathering with the Holy Spirit is priceless. It is always filled with love, joy, and understanding. It always leaves me with His inspired Will to start my day with assurance.

I entered the room and opened my Bible. I started turning the pages, and I flipped right to the Scriptures regarding Shadrach, Meshach, and Abednego, which I had just read a couple of weeks ago. This time, it was different because I immediately flipped right to it. Because I went right to this Scripture, I knew there was something the Spirit of the Lord wanted me to know. So I began to read it.

When I came to verse 27 in Daniel 3 (AKJV), it said, "And the princes, governors, and captains, and the king's counsellors, being gathered together, saw these men, upon whose bodies the fire had no power, nor was an hair of their head singed, neither were their coats changed, nor the smell of fire had passed on them."

After reading the Scripture, the Spirit of the Lord stopped me and encouraged me to meditate on the part that says, "The fire had no power."

Then the Spirit of the Lord began to tell me that all of the things that bothered me had no power—the way people would speak to me in a derogatory way or they rejected me, my feelings of not measuring up, and all of my insecurities—there is no power in any of them. He said that all power is in the Holy Spirit and His truth, not in the things of the world.

I personally thank You, Holy Spirit, for giving Your Word of truth, making me free, renewing my mind, and making a new season for me that is bright in You.

Hebrews 11:34 (NASB): ... quenched the power of fire, escaped the edge of the sword, from weakness were made strong, became mighty in war, put foreign armies to flight.

106

Stolen tag brought forgiveness

I had clocked out from work about 6:10 p.m. only to encounter a surprise as I approached my car. No license tag! It was absolutely gone! I stood there for a few minutes in awe that someone had stolen my tag. This had never happened to me before.

I lowered my bags to the ground and called my husband, informing him what had happened and that I had no license plate on the car. After listening to his instructions, I hung up and called the police. It took them a while to arrive at the scene, but once they arrived, they were kind and got right on the case.

They said someone had used professional tools to remove the tag, and they were able to do it very quickly. They gave me a report to take to the State Licensing office to report a stolen tag and to get a new tag.

As I was driving home, I thought I would be nervous driving without a tag and possibly being stopped by the police. But there was a peaceful protection that consoled me.

When I arrived home, I asked my husband not to mention this to anyone because I had forgiven the person who did it. I felt a sincere, deep compassion for the person who stole the license plate.

I went into my prayer room, got down on my knees, and praised the Lord for His love that endures forever, thanking Him for choosing me first. I know you may ask what this has to do with someone stealing my tag, but I thought about all of the times that Jesus has forgiven me for my misdeeds and how He continues to see me through His love. Why not express the same love for someone else who may one day ask for forgiveness and open the door for Jesus Christ to come into his life. I expressed to my Savior that I wanted to be pleasing in His sight and for my heart to stay renewed in Him.

Hallelujah!

---

1 John 4:17 (NLT): And as we live in God, our love grows more perfect. So we will not be afraid on the day of judgment, but we can face him with confidence because we live like Jesus here in this world.

107

Guilt blinded, love made me see

Today, for the first time, I realized Trina has taken me out for my birthday for the past 15 years or more. For years, I had a happy but sad feeling when Trina would take me out. I had a limited income, and there was not much I could do for her when her birthday came around.

I used to think Trina took me out because she felt sorry for me. I do not know how I came up with that mindset. I could not see Trina taking me out for my birthday out of love.

Now I know that my own thoughts deceived me and blinded me with guilt because of my circumstances. I allowed a limited income to put me into fear. I thought if I could not do something for Trina's birthday, then she would not know that I loved her, too. My own guilt robbed me of the joy she intentionally gave to me personally on my birthday.

When Trina took me out to eat on my last birthday, it was different. My heart was renewed with love because I had received understanding that Trina never expected to receive anything from me for her birthday.

This time I saw that it truly brought her joy to spend time with me on my birthday as she always has, and this time I saw it plainly.

I could see that for all of these years as my birthday approached, Trina intentionally made special time for me, making sure my day was bright and full of love.

Acts 20:35 (ESV): "… In all things I have shown you that by working hard in this way we must help the weak and remember the words of the Lord Jesus, how he himself said, 'It is more blessed to give than to receive.'"

108

Everlasting is peace

The Spirit of the Lord said to me, "I give you things to richly enjoy, not to give you peace through them." There was a time when my thoughts were, "If I had everything I needed and wanted, I would surely have peace."

My lesson was learned when we bought our first home. I remembered that long ago, when my son and I lived in an apartment in Virginia, I had a picture of a beautiful house taped on my mirror in my bedroom. My son remembers those times very well.

So, when my husband and I bought our first home, I was full of joy and at peace, or so I thought. I did not realize that I had no clue what peace really was because my peace seemed to be unstable while living in that home.

I had thought that owning my own home would bring peace. I also found temporary pleasure in having a home improvement business. There was nothing wrong with the home or the business. The problem was thinking that a worldly possession or business could bring peace.

Then I embraced the truth of God's Word when He said, "True peace is only in Him and not in the world." How can something that is constantly changing and diminishing give you peace? Impossible! God's peace is the same yesterday, today, and forever.

His peace has no attachment to the world that is passing away. Therefore, through His Word, I can count on God's peace for love, salvation, protection, correction, and righteousness without hesitation.

John 14:27 (ESV): Peace I leave with you; my peace I give to you. Not as the world gives do I give to you. Let not your hearts be troubled, neither let them be afraid.

109

Promotion in a fiery furnace

I am learning not to fear things men try to put on me that oppose God's Word. No matter how things seem at the time, obedience to God's Word should be done boldly when tested by someone who goes against Him.

We must completely trust in what His Word declares. We must obey the Spirit of Truth whether we are delivered or not. Shadrach, Meshach, and Abednego boldly declared, "… we do not need to defend ourselves before you. If we are thrown into the blazing furnace, the God whom we serve is able to save us. He will rescue us from your power, Your Majesty. But even if he doesn't, we want to make it clear to you, Your Majesty, that we will never serve your gods or worship the gold statue you have set up" (Daniel 38:16b-18 NLT).

And, perhaps, as Nebuchadnezzar witnessed and was changed, others will witness the salvation of the Lord and be changed through those who boldly stand up for Who we believe.

Shadrach, Meshach, and Abednego were great examples for us to model with their boldness in seeking to honor God and not men. In seeking to honor God, men will honor my God and me as Nebuchadnezzar did with Shadrach, Meshach and Abednego. And because Shadrach, Meshach, and Abednego honored God, Nebuchadnezzar promoted them.

I know through experience that to be promoted is not to seek to please men but to honor and please Jesus Christ alone. Our King of kings, and Lord of lords, who knows the minds and hearts of everyone knows exactly how to deliver and promote us in the midst of any fiery furnace.

Hallelujah!

Daniel 3:28-30 (NLT): Then Nebuchadnezzar said, "Praise to the God of Shadrach, Meshach, and Abednego! He sent his angel to rescue his servants who trusted in him. They defied the king's command and were willing to die rather than serve or worship any god except their own God. Therefore, I make this decree: If any people, whatever their race or nation or language, speak a word against the God of Shadrach, Meshach, and Abednego, they will be torn limb from limb, and their houses will be turned into heaps of rubble. There is no other god who can rescue like this!" Then the king promoted Shadrach, Meshach, and Abednego to even higher positions in the province of Babylon.

110

Loving from a renewed heart

The Spirit of the Lord brought this to me in my praise and worship. "Loving your mother from a renewed heart in Him is more important than when you knew her before it was renewed."

I thought about what He said, and peace took hold of me. My relationship with Jesus changed my relationship with my mother. My love for her now is pure and genuine. It had not been that way before.

Looking back, I had put a lot of the blame on my mother. But the Spirit of the Lord corrected. The blame lay in the way my heart was conformed to the world's way of thinking. And, believe me, my way of worldly thinking spoke loud and clear, imprisoning me in deceit of the way I used to feel about my mother.

The Word of the Lord pulled down every stronghold that held me captive against loving my mother. I am truly grateful for the Holy Spirit Who speaks to me always, transforming my heart and making His light shine through me to show the true love I have through Christ Jesus!

Romans 12:2 (ESV): Do not be conformed to this world, but be transformed by the renewal of your mind, that by testing you may discern what is the will of God, what is good and acceptable and perfect.

111

Christ Jesus, our high position

I have always equated being in a high position as having a career. However, having a renewed mind and knowing the truth in Christ Jesus changed my view and my life's journey.

There is no higher position than being in Christ Jesus, the One Who created heaven and earth and everything in it. It is incredible how different the thoughts are when looking through the eyes of the Holy Spirit than when looking through the eyes of the world.

A changed heart with a love to please Christ set my heart thermometer to a perfect temperature. Living, moving, and having my being in Christ Jesus is a high position. Why would anyone choose being a part of this world, accepting a low position, and losing the soul? Can we not see that the world is fading right before our eyes?

I choose my Father in Christ Jesus, Who is Creator of everything, with all power, all glory, all might, and it all belongs to Him. I choose eternal life with Christ Jesus because the highest position EVER is in Him! Hallelujah!!

James 1:9 (NASB): But the brother of humble circumstances is to glory in his high position …

112

Opportunities begin with repentance

The Spirit of the Lord dropped His wisdom in my ear while I was eating. He said, "Angela, you have asked in the past for Me to open up doors of opportunity for you to witness and lay hands on the sick. I want you to take serious heed to what I am about to say.

"From the time you started believing in My Name when you repented and turned to Me, opportunities began right at that moment. Every place you have walked had opportunities to heal the sick and tell of the Good News about Me. You never have to ask for opportunities that are commanded of you in My Word. GO! I AM with you!"

Mark 16:15 (NLT): And then he told them, "Go into all the world and preach the Good News to everyone …"

Jude 1:23 (ESV): … save others by snatching them out of the fire; to others show mercy with fear, hating even the garment stained by the flesh.

113

Jesus is exceedingly more

A couple of weeks ago, I was concerned about doing business alone in one of our tents for a festival with "It's Gotta B Lemonade." This was the first time my husband and I would be in two separate tents for a festival selling his most famous organic juiced lemonades, with over 100 different fresh juiced fruits and vegetables.

I have always felt uncomfortable being bombarded with people at our booth while taking orders and handling money. I would rather fill the order and let someone else take the order and handle the money. I get too overwhelmed by the crowd when I am up front. I am most comfortable handling business in the back.

As the day was approaching, I felt more and more nervous about the situation. Then suddenly, I stopped and said to myself, "Angela, you have a Father Who is the same today as He was yesterday and all those other days He has helped you."

I started to remember and speak out all the times the Holy Spirit helped, rescued, gave, and so much more. This situation was no different because Christ Jesus is the same Helper as He was in times past.

In communion with my Father, I poured out my concern about my fear of being bombarded with so many people at our booth table while taking orders, handling money, and then filling the orders. After I poured out my concern to the Lord, I told Him I would leave it with Him. This was three days prior to the event.

Then, with conviction, I reminded my Heavenly Father about His Word, asking Him to do what He has said. I reminded Him that He said He would help me, He would uphold me and strengthen me with His righteous right hand. Then I gave Him His Word that He had given to me, that I would not fear, and I ended it there.

After communing with Christ Jesus, He consoled me with His love and peace. I had asked Mia if she would help me in the tent at the festival, and she said yes. Mia came and brought her daughter, Emily, to help also.

While we were still getting things together in the tent, Emily walked to the other tent where my husband Elliott was working. I was about to ask Mia if she would handle the money, but before I could get it out, she said, "Angela, I'm going to let you handle the money." I told her I was just about to ask her if she would handle the money, and we both burst out laughing. So I stated that we would ask Emily if she would handle the money. Mia agreed and replied, "Yeah, we'll ask her," as we continued to laugh.

When Emily returned from the other booth, I asked her if she would do the cashiering. With excitement, she said, "Sure." Emily put a big smile on my face, and she did not even know it. I was so grateful. When customers came to the booth, Mia took their orders and handled the lemonade, and Emily collected the money. The Lord kept me in His perfect peace in the booth until I was able to handle all the transactions required to keep customers happy.

Then Christ Jesus did exceedingly more than I had asked for. When I looked over to my left, there came Sophia with her husband, Jacob, who was helping my husband out at the other booth. When I saw Sophia coming toward me I was filled with joy and approached her with open arms of appreciation that she had come to help me.

As soon as Sophia entered the booth, she jumped right in and started helping with everything. Christ Jesus helped me exceedingly above what I had asked for, and I am forever grateful to Him and my family.

Hallelujah!

Psalm 34:17 (NLT): The LORD hears his people when they call him for help. He rescues them from all their troubles.

Ephesians 3:20 (ESV): Now to him who is able to do far more abundantly than all that we ask or think, according to the power at work within us ...

Epilogue

I live my life abiding in the Holy Spirit Who gives me wonderful experiences daily. I am not perfect, but in Him, He gives me perfect experiences to exemplify Who He is in me and, at the same time, to show His light to others.

---

1 John 4:17 **(ONM):** By this, love has been made complete among us, so that we would have fearless confidence in the Day of Judgment, because just as that One is, we ourselves are like Him in this world.

About the Author

ANGELA SCOTT SIMPSON

ANGELA SCOTT SIMPSON grew up in a small town in Florida. She was raised attending church and was very active in the choir, plays, Bible studies, fundraisers, and of course, Sunday school. Her mom was a Sunday school teacher, and there was no chance of missing church. Angela experienced ongoing revivals, not quite understanding what revivals were all about, but the people seemed to be having a joyful time in the Lord and in fellowship with believers from other churches.

As Angela was maturing in age, she became aware that she lacked understanding in the Word of God. She would read, and it was as if she was reading something strange. Although Angela heard the Word over and over in church, something was not right, and she did not understand why there was a blockage. This was beginning to puzzle her greatly because she had a deep desire to understand the Word of God.

In her thirties, Angela repented and began asking the Holy Spirit to give her a deeper understanding of His Word and to help her be a doer of the Word. God began an intimate work in her heart, preparing her for a Kingdom future with Him.

Angela's journey with the Holy Spirit has led to a heartfelt desire to share God's love. Her prayer is that others may experience His presence, hear His voice, and be assured of everlasting life with the Lord Jesus Christ through their own journey with the Holy Spirit.